P9-BIJ-031

THERE'S NO BUSINESS LIKE GOD'S BUSINESS

THERE'S NO BUSINESS LIKE GOD'S BUSINESS

Chuck Murphy

Nashville - ABINGDON PRESS - New York

THERE'S NO BUSINESS LIKE GOD'S BUSINESS

Copyright © 1974 by Abingdon Press

All rights in this book are reserved.
No part of this book may be reproduced in any
manner whatsoever without written permission of
the publishers except brief quotations embodied in
critical articles or reviews. For information address
Abingdon Press, Nashville, Tennessee.

Library of Congress Cataloging in Publication Data

MURPHY, CHUCK, 1922-
There's no business like God's business.

1. Theology, Doctrinal—Popular works. 2. Christian
life—Anglican authors. I. Title.
BT77.M92   248'.48'3   73-20312

ISBN 0-687-41632-9

Scripture quotations are from the Revised Standard
Version of the Bible, copyrighted 1946, 1952, and
1972 by the Division of Christian Education, National
Council of Churches, and are used by permission.

MANUFACTURED BY THE PARTHENON PRESS AT
NASHVILLE, TENNESSEE, UNITED STATES OF AMERICA

This book is dedicated to my wife, Anne, to my children, Donna, Chuck, Tim, Katy, and Chris, and to my mother-in-law, Mrs. J. R. Hunter. They have always been my rooting section. My family "went to college and seminary" with me in more ways than one. Without their prayers, love, encouragement, and cooperation my ministry would be so much less satisfying to me, and less effective with other people.

FOREWORD

The prophet Habukkuk wrote, "Write the vision; make plain it upon tablets, so he may run who reads it." Chuck Murphy, writer with a sense of urgency and a kind of holy restlessness for this fast-paced world of ours, writes as he speaks—quickly, plainly, and clearly.

The content of the book is based upon Fr. Murphy's highly successful Teaching Missions which have enabled countless people to appropriate the abundant life that Jesus offers. In essence his message is not new—it is "the old, old story of Jesus and His love." But it is presented in new and fresh ways, marked by the author's deep sense of aliveness and his loving appreciation of humor.

The great asset of the book lies perhaps in his explicit and direct presentation of the Good News using only the most basic and unpretentious words of our language. This is verbal communication at its best and its value will be reflected in the reader having to respond either "yes" or "no." Father Murphy does not allow us the luxury of dodging the issue by saying "I don't understand."

The seeker and the believer will find here much that is helpful, and in particular the author's treatment of salvation. From childhood we have been imbued with the "work ethic"—that which is good must be earned. This notion is so deep within us that while we profess with our lips an absolute belief in salvation by faith, our actions clearly indicate that our true belief is salvation by works. With clear preciseness he cuts to the core of the matter with such statements as, "we may be 'good' because we have been saved, but we are not saved because we are 'good.'" Such preciseness as this occurs again and again. It reaches its zenith when he turns to the subject of judgment and tells us that God will have only one word to address to each of us. I will not reveal the word here because I want you to savor the profoundness and the humor of this thought within its context.

Father Murphy questions our false gods and is not afraid of arriving at ideas and solutions that will offend some and cause pain to others. He is a man of courage who loves life and whose whole thinking is based on his concern that all persons may have the opportunity to claim the new life that is their rightful inheritance in Christ Jesus. The importance of his thoughts lies in the fact that they can have a freeing effect on the heart and the mind by showing entirely new possibilities; and they can make the reader more alive because they open the door that leads out of the prison of self into the glorious freedom of the children of God.

Furman C. Stough
Bishop of Alabama

CONTENTS

PREFACE

"THERE'S NO BUSINESS LIKE SHOW BUSINESS, THERE'S NO BUSINESS I KNOW" is the first line of a song by Irving Berlin that has become the unofficial theme song for the entertainment world. This was a philosophy that I believed years before Mr. Berlin wrote his song—and some fifteen years afterwards. From the time I was eight or nine years old and heard the applause following a song that I had just played and sung, I was hooked on show biz. Piano recitals, amateur nights at the local movie theatre, and performing at school assembly programs confirmed me in my belief. Playing and singing in the local dance orchestra and performing on the local radio station helped to prepare me for what I was convinced was my calling in life. This early beginning led to a career recording for Coral, Columbia, and MGM record companies, three years of daily TV programs in Birmingham, Alabama, and nightclub engagements in Hollywood, Texas, Oklahoma, Canada, and on the East Coast. My modestly successful show business career gave me adequate financial rewards, "ego trips" from recognition and approval, and oddly enough, a happy family life. Although I enjoyed being an entertainer and still like to entertain and hear the intoxicating sound of applause, I began to realize when I was in my early thirties that show business was not quite, for me, the ultimate in living.

The more involved I became in my local church, the less satisfying and important my lifelong musical career became. Then one day when my minister in an offhand remark suggested that perhaps I ought to enter the ministry, the seed was planted. I was intrigued but thought the idea was ridiculous because I had not had any college whatsoever. The more my wife and I thought about it, the more we became fascinated with the idea. After quite a bit of prayer, I began to investigate just what would be required. We finally decided to give it a try, and although I had a wife and five children, I entered college as a freshman at the age of thirty-five. I continued to support my family by playing at a private club at night with my musical combo, but I was on my way toward eventually entering seminary to study for the Episcopal ministry.

As a latecomer to the ministry, I can truthfully say that I have found a much better, more exciting, and more satisfying business. At the same time I am convinced that "there is no business like God's business, there's no business I know" that has been more misunderstood, misinterpreted, misused, and ineffectively conducted in many, many instances. Were it not God's business, with the Holy Spirit actively involved, it would have closed down many centuries ago. I know that neither the gates of hell nor the sinfulness of man can destroy God's business, the Church; but man has certainly hindered the work of the Church and blocked many people from enjoying the life God wants for his loved ones. Man's sinfulness is greatly responsible, but incorrect information—implied or actually stated—plus failure to teach on the part of the church, has served to hinder the real work of the Church and to prevent man from fulfilling God's original purpose for him. I believe this to be one of, if not the greatest, tragedies of all time.

This book is the result of eighty-nine "Teaching Missions" conducted in three different denominations and nine states. The size of the various groups has varied from some twenty-five to over two hundred and twenty-five people. Three of them have been for teen-agers, but the rest have been composed of people of all ages and many denominations. Although these Teaching Missions have been held only in Methodist, Presbyterian, and Episcopal churches, there have been people from almost every Christian denomination in attendance. I do not believe that I have heard a new question since the third one of these that I have conducted. Adults ask the same questions as young people, and most of them have the same misconceptions and hang-ups about Christianity. Since these missions are on basic Christianity and not Episcopalianism per se, we have seldom gotten into doctrinal differences, regardless of the denominational make-up of the groups.

I am convinced that the majority of church members do not know the basics of Christianity. This was certainly true for me, even though I was a regular, and involved, Christian layman long before I ever gave any thought about becoming a minister. Most laymen do not know the meanings of many important religious terms, and neither do they understand what the benefits and responsibilities of being a Christian are. Any other business in the world that had workers so uniformed and so poorly equipped would have closed up shop in less than one year's time.

One could never expect to be a successful doctor, lawyer, salesman, engineer, and the like, unless he knew and understood the basic terms, expectations, assets, and requirements for that profession. Yet, many Christians attempt to be good, successful Christians without knowing and understanding the basics of the lifelong business of conducting the mission and ministry of Christianity's founder, Jesus Christ. It surely must be the pure grace of God that has prevented the spiritual bankruptcy of his business.

I never fail to be amazed at the way God works. Oddly enough, these Teaching Missions had their origin in a program in which I participated that took a completely opposite approach in presenting the Christian faith. I attended a three-phased Leadership Training Institute in Avon Park, Florida. Phase one was a week spent in intensive group life where the participants were trained in the skills of sensitivity toward one another. Phase two was a ten-day session of this T-group life, one month later, where the techniques of being sensitive toward others were put into theoretical situations, and finally, phase three was an actual back-home program in a real life situation.

Shortly before leaving for Avon Park I was contacted by a group of women from a nearby small church who asked if I would come and help them develop something that would aid them in maintaining some kind of active church life while they were waiting for a new minister to be sent to them. I suggested to three members of our training group that we make this our "back home" project. They agreed, and we arranged for a three-night meeting with the people in that church so that we could attempt to apply our newly learned skills.

The first night one of our group began to explain the Christian faith in a well-thought-out academic way, and after a little while one man in the church broke in with, "What in the world has all this got to do with helping St. John's?" To put it kindly, our first night was a flop—and yet, it was no one's fault. It was as if they either did not understand the Christian faith, or at least they didn't see where it had a great deal to do with "keeping the church open" while they waited for another "professional" Christian to come and carry on the church's business.

Driving back home to the town where I was pastor of a church, we were a pretty depressed quartet who didn't know what we would do for our second act. As we rode along trying to come up with some idea, one of the ministers, who was chaplain at Auburn University at the time, recalled that I had recently preached a sermon at Auburn on basically the same subject that had been presented that night. He suggested that the next night I preach the same sermon in a dialogue manner, and perhaps the people at St. John's would see that it had everything to do with "keeping the church open" and conducting God's business. Since we had come up with no other alternatives, I agreed to give it a try the next night. Presenting the Christian truths in a down to earth manner apparently made more sense than the same truths couched in theological terms. Evidence of this was seen in the fact that the reaction of some of the people attending the meeting the next night

15

was completely different. For some of them, their eyes were opened for the first time to the relationship of Christianity and the everyday business of being the people of God.

Shortly after that, another small church contacted the state headquarters of our denomination concerning some help in keeping their church active and interest alive while they were waiting for a new minister to come, and it was suggested that I go and do pretty much the same thing there that we had used for our phase three in the other small church. I asked another minister to go with me, with the idea that I would do the presentation and he would handle the question and answer portion. This seemed to work well, and shortly afterwards a third church asked me to come and conduct the same type of three-night meeting. That time I asked still another minister to participate in it with me. After that I conducted them alone for two reasons: one, it is much harder for two ministers to arrange to go than one, and two, most of the questions were directed toward me since I was the one whose presentation triggered the questions and comments.

I believe that Christianity is the most EXCITING life that it is possible to live, but so few people enjoy its benefits and accept its responsibilities because they have not been taught, or at least, they have failed to learn what Christianity really is.

This book is primarily the content of my three-night Teaching Missions. There is little, if anything, new in it, but because of the basic theological ignorance of most church people, they quite often respond as if it were something brand new that I had personally concocted.

It is Christian doctrine that I believe is found in the Gospels and Epistles of the New Testament, particularly the letters of St. Paul. The facts and thoughts that I try to get across come from so many different sources that it would be impossible for me to give credit to those I learned them from.

Of course, part of my theology comes from some of my professors at The Virginia Seminary, but the books of Sam Shoemaker, Carrol E. Simcox, Louis Cassels, Watchman Nee, John Huess, and many, many others have played their part in coloring it. I imagine that every minister puts together his Christian theology from many sources, and the final result becomes, in a sense, uniquely his—but there is only one Christian message, and it comes from the words, deeds, and person of Jesus Christ.

I am indebted to Mr. and Mrs. Ira West who let me and my family use their guest house in Gulf Shores, Alabama, during the summer of 1972, where I could put this book down in rough form.

I am indebted to Dr. and Mrs. Abraham Cheij of Nashville, Tennessee who read it, and especially to Mrs. Cheij who laboriously corrected my many mistakes of grammar and punctuation.

I am also indebted to the many hundreds of people who attended my Teaching Missions and helped me to formulate it through their questions and comments.

I hope that anyone who reads this will find some help in what I intended to be a simple explanation of what the Christian faith and life is all about.

Chapter One

MAN'S PREDICAMENT

DECATUR

The more staid and self-righteous Presbyterians, Methodists, Episcopalians, Baptists . . . were shocked into sober thoughtfulness Tuesday night when "that crazy Episcopalian" minister from Birmingham gave them the "bad news."

Rev. Charles (Chuck) Murphy, former Decaturite who was a nightclub entertainer 18 years before his ordination at 41, is in Decatur to conduct another of his unique "teaching missions" at Westminster Presbyterian Church.

Some in the audience knew "Chuck", since he grew up in Decatur, but even so some were no doubt stunned when, opening the session, Chuck (wearing his clerical collar) promptly sat down at the piano and accompanying himself, led the group in a rousing round of choruses.

"I got a home in Gloryland that outshines the sun," he sang in his former stage career style, and it was evident that Mr. Murphy knew how to loosen his audience for the "dialogue" which was to follow his short message.

Getting up from the piano, Rev. Murphy said, "Let us pray: Heavenly Father, open our hearts, our minds and help us to see ourselves in our true relationship to You. May Your Holy Spirit take control of this gathering." The sudden turn of atmosphere had its effect.

This excerpt from an article in *The Decatur* (Alabama) *Daily* accurately describes a typical beginning of my Teaching Mission.

I am sure that it is difficult for people who had known me as a stagestruck kid and have followed my career in the entertainment field to see me now as a minister. All of us, at one time or another, have had a stereotyped picture of a minister. When people see and hear me playing the piano, clapping my hands, and singing, their ministerial image is shaken. My own preconceived ideas concerning preachers prevented me from even considering the ministry as a vocation for many years. I finally realized that when God calls you to participate in his business, he does not take away any talents you had when you were in some other business. Talents are a gift from God, and he enhances those talents when you use them for him. My Teaching Missions are one way that I try to show people the excitement and the joy that I have found in turning more of my life over to Jesus Christ. To be a committed Christian is to be a partner in God's business. There's no business like God's business because every other business operates on the reward system, while God's business offers free, unmerited grace from the first moment you enter it. The rewards are great, but they are entirely unearned. They are a part of the new kind of life that Jesus gives.

In going about God's business, twelve men took up a crusade which overturned the Roman Empire—a crusade that changed lives, cultures, and history. Today, millions of people claim to belong to that same crusade. Why hasn't that crusade changed the world even more during the past twenty centuries? Why are not more people living the life

Jesus Christ inaugurated? Why are so many people who bear the name "Christian" missing out on the new life Christ promised—and delivered? There are many who are living that life, enjoying its benefits and accepting its responsibilities; but in proportion to the number who merely bear the name, but miss the life, the number is tragically small. If this were not so, the churches would be filled to overflowing and the lives of Christians would be such a witness that Christianity would be having as startling an impact on the twentieth century as it had on the first century.

Many people honestly believe that Christianity has failed, or at least is ineffective. Even for some people who are technically "Christian," it has little real meaning. It is saddening to realize how many Christians are merely existing, when they were meant to "live." It is saddening to find frustrated, despairing Christians who are missing out on the joy that could be theirs. I believe this is so because they have failed to associate Christianity with life. They have not found Christianity to be the life-changing experience that it can be—and is meant to be. For many Christians, the church seems to be something you "do" occasionally on Sundays. I have heard it said that many English people believe that it is important that one belong to a church, but you only attend three times: to be hatched, matched, and dispatched. For them, the church exists so that one can be baptized, married, and buried respectably. Even if this is an exaggeration, the fact that such a statement can be made signifies that something has happened to or gone out of that vital, on-fire organism that was born on Pentecost approximately nineteen hundred and forty years ago. What happened to the original zeal? Where is the exciting kind of life Jesus came to bring? Why is much of the organized church made up of "in-name-only" Christians who neither enjoy the benefits nor accept the responsibilities of being members of the Body of Christ, the Church? Without having to repeat it ever so often, let me say again that there are quite a few Christians who are enjoying those benefits and have accepted the responsibilities and who are living the abundant life. My concern is with the question of why are not all Christians doing so.

I am convinced that many Christians do not really know and understand what Christianity is and that they never will until something happens. Many lifelong members who attend church services regularly have never "heard" the Good News of Christianity because they have never realized the bad news of their situation. Of course there are some who have heard the bad news and have gone no farther. They have stopped there and just given up. This is just as great a tragedy as never hearing the good news. This good news is indispensible for living life the way God planned it, but until a person understands the bad news of his situation, he is not ready to hear the Good News of Jesus Christ. To try to explain this it helps to recall the story of Adam and Eve in the Garden of Eden. Not because it is the first thing in the Bible, but because it is the story of you and me —today. It was not written as history, but to point out what we are like and to describe our situation. It reflects the way man cuts himself off from God by declaring his independence, and trying to run his own life—be his own god.

In creation, God gave us the great gift of freedom. This gift is the third greatest gift he has given us, after Jesus

21

Christ and the Holy Spirit, but it is also our greatest problem. It is the cause of our downfall. We can say "no" to God. We can shake our fist in his face, we can curse him . . . and he won't strike us dead. I used to think he would, but he won't. We are free—otherwise, we would be robots; and robots have no freedom, and they also have no life. One cannot have a real relationship with a robot. God wanted a love relationship between himself and man, but such a love relationship is possible only when each part is free to respond or refuse. If your children have to love you, their love will be of no value. The only love that is love, and worth anything, is love that is voluntarily given. It is no different between God and man.

According to the story, Adam and Eve had it "knocked" as far as life was concerned. Everything was perfect; everything was provided—no worries, no problems. There was only one thing that marred their perfect existence. God had placed one restriction—one limitation. This was one too many. Man misused his freedom and rebelled against God. He disobeyed God, and messed things up. This misuse of freedom has been man's problem from the very beginning. Understanding this is fundamental to the growth of a mature person. In order to grow toward the right relationship with God, we must understand what sin is—and understand it in a way that hits home in our lives. I believe the meaning of sin is one of the most misunderstood aspects of religion and life. Without understanding its full meaning, we will not be able to understand the Good News.

I was born in 1922 and grew up in a small southern town in the buckle of the Bible Belt. The religious culture at the time was one that seemed to concentrate on sins with a little "s." In those days before TV, revivals were big events. Nearly everyone attended, and it didn't matter much which denomination was holding the revival. They were social as well as religious gatherings. You either took a date, or "picked up" a date, and the revivals provided a place to go, and something to do. They didn't have to—and often didn't—have much lasting effect on one's life. As a teen-ager whose religious life centered primarily around "gimmie" prayers to a Santa Claus-type God, my reaction to the content of these revivals was not too favorable. All I remember about them was some screaming preacher telling me, "Don't smoke, drink, dance, play cards, go to movies, etc." There was nothing much that came through to me that attracted me to what came over as the Christian life. I was a nominal Christian with little understanding of the real meaning of Christianity. I was saturated with the "do's" and "don't's" of preaching. The wrath of God was held like a big stick over my head, but I don't remember hearing much about his love. It seemed to me that he was "up there" keeping a record of how bad I was and just waiting to give me a failing mark on my religious report card. I do not recall hearing much about the here and now benefits of Christianity, and I saw little evidence of them in the lives of people who were supposed to be very religious. I saw a great deal of joyless "holier-than-thou" church people. It seemed to me that life was something "religious" folk were to endure, and if they denied themselves enough, one day "in the sweet bye and bye," God would reward them by not sending them to a burning hell, but would allow them to enter heaven. Somehow, to a teen-ager, this was not very appealing. I don't think this is appealing to anyone, ever. I also do not believe that this is a very effective approach for coming into a love relationship with God.

It seemed to me that religion concentrated on these sins with a little "s." I am not very concerned with these—if indeed they are sins. I believe that you can make a sin out of anything. But, when they are sins, they are just manifestations of SIN, with a capital "S"—which is a state, not a deed. There are two words that label sin: INORDINATE PRIDE. There is nothing wrong with pride. Without it there would be little culture or progress, but inordinate pride is pride out of order. As an attempt to explain this, let us take inordinate love—love out of order. When I love a person the way I am supposed to love God—this is love out of order. When I love an animal the way I should love people, this is love out of order. Inordinate love for anything distorts the wonderful thing called love, and often becomes obsession. Pride, in order, is necessary and desirable.

Self-respect is admirable, and civilization would deteriorate without pride, but inordinate pride is obsession with SELF. It means putting self at the center of everything. It means trying to make the world revolve around *you*. It is making one's self "old number one"—ahead of anything or anybody, including God. This is sin, and it is a state that manifests itself in deeds. I have known preachers whose theology was primarily based on "Thou shalt not drink." It is just as sinful to overeat as it is to overdrink. I have spent a great deal of my life overeating. If I continue to do so, I am liable to die early. This will deprive my children of a father, my wife of a husband—at least, temporarily; and if I am doing God's work, it will cut it short. The immediate results of overdrinking can be greater than from overeating, but they are both due to sin. The same thing that causes overdrinking causes overeating. It is doing what one wants to do no matter whom it may hurt. It is the exaltation of self. This is "original sin." I used to think that original sin was sex, but it isn't—although it may express itself in the misuse of sex. Original sin is something that we are born with.

I like to use the example of a baby. A baby doesn't care if you have to kill someone to get him his milk—he wants his milk. A baby doesn't care how inconvenient it is for you to get out of a nice bed in the middle of the night in order to change him when he is wet—he wants to be comfortable. Now, I know that a baby doesn't know any better, and that there is a certain element of self-preservation that is absolutely necessary, but the point is that a baby is completely self-centered. Self-centeredness is what original sin is. It is more than just selfishness, it is complete self-centeredness. This is something we are born with and something that sticks with us forever, unless something happens to change our nature. As a baby grows, his self-centeredness remains, and may even increase, if possible.

As the father of four children out of the teen-age years and one still in his teens, I feel qualified to say that inordinate pride reaches a pretty high plateau during the teen years. I also remember myself at that age. Most of us remember what a devastating effect a new pimple can have on a teen-ager. A new bit of acne can make his or her world seem to crash in, but—as self-centered as most teen-agers are—I am convinced that some of the most completely self-

25

centered people in the world are in their sixties, seventies, and eighties. I had an aunt who was this way. You could tell her about someone you know having cancer, and she would say, "Isn't that too bad, but you don't know what trouble is until your teeth don't fit right"—and she was dead serious because her false teeth never fit.

What many people call sins are mere by-products of this fundamental sin. Lying, stealing, murder, and all the other things that are called sins are manifestations of the one sin, self-centeredness. For example, why do people lie? Distorting the truth is done in order to protect one's self from blame or hurt. People lie in order to profit materially or with the hope of gaining admiration or recognition. Many people lie to protect or gain something for those they love —but even this is basically for self.

I believe that gossip is one of the greatest and most common manifestations of sin. Have you ever noticed how little we gossip about the good things people do? We may say, "Wasn't such-and-such a thing nice . . . but, did you hear . . . ? Then we get to the juicy part. You see, somehow or another, if I can say something, perhaps ever so subtly, that tears you and your reputation down, it subconsciously seems to build me and my reputation up. Character assassination is as serious in God's eyes as murder is in man's. What I am really saying when I gossip is, "I don't do that sort of thing, and he does. I'm nicer than he is."

It is possible that you may have some special kind of sin that I have never heard of, but I don't believe it is possible for it not to have its origin in inordinate pride. Sins come from this obsession with self. This self-love takes many forms. For example, our reaction to criticism: our hurt feelings. Love is at its most ecstatic when mutual acceptance is greatest. I personally do not believe that, for me, there is any such thing as constructive criticism. I take a very dim view of criticism of any kind. Having spent many years in show business before entering the ministry, I need constant approval and acceptance. I am positive that this is the reason many people go into show business. They need approval, acceptance, and praise almost as much as they need food, water, and air.

Possessiveness, "smother love," and the will-to-power are other examples of inordinate pride. Most of us have known, or known about, people who rule entire families from a sickbed. Just cross them about anything, and they take to their beds with heart attacks or migraine headaches. They recover remarkably when they finally get their way. Trouble comes when two self-centered people meet head-on. When a child is most helpless and dependent, tenderness toward it is at a maximum—this is an ego-builder, but just let that rotten kid get old enough to want to do what he wants, instead of what I want him to do, and something other than tenderness tends to creep in.

Just so we realize that no one escapes: we know that a conceited person is self-centered, but it is important that we also realize that a person with an inferiority complex is just as self-centered as one who is conceited. A person with an inferiority complex doesn't think very highly of himself—but, he thinks *about* himself all the time. During my Teaching Missions I always mention that many of the people there will not open their mouths during the dialogue periods of the three nights because they do not want to speak unless they can say something brilliant or because

27

they do not want other people to realize that they didn't know something or other. This is not being modest. It is being self-centered. Actually, no one escapes from this original sin of self-centeredness unless something drastic happens to him.

This is the cause of all the trouble in the world between people. Any kind of trouble in relationships comes from this one thing. It is the cause of all the trouble between husbands and wives, parents and children, labor and management. It is the cause of trouble between the races and between nations. Trouble between people is caused by the individual or corporate self-centeredness of people.

Because we all have this inordinate pride—we all want our way and want the world to revolve around ourselves—people, individually and corporately, have fought, struggled, and killed one another. Because of this sin we find ourselves estranged from God, our fellowman, and even ourselves.

Many centuries ago, we were given the Ten Commandments. Later on, these were capsuled into what is called "The Summary of the Law"; "Thou shalt love the Lord thy God with all thy heart, with all thy soul and with all thy mind, and thou shalt love thy neighbor as thyself." We acknowledge this easily, but I do not think that we really understand what it means. This means that every minute of my life God is to come first—ahead of everything, including myself. Twenty-four hours a day God and his will must come first in my thoughts and my deeds, and you, and everyone I meet, are to be loved by me the same way I love myself. THIS IS GOD'S REQUIREMENT. I am supposed to do this, and when I don't—God and I are separated. Do you really understand the enormity of this demand? I can't even stay on a diet. How on earth can I keep such an impossible demand as the Summary of the Law?

I grew up thinking, and many people still do, that God keeps a scoreboard. You know: 9,768 "goods" and 9,769 "bads"; and he says, "Sorry, but I've got to send you to hell. You just missed it by one." You may laugh, but this idea is in the back of many people's minds. This is ridiculous. We cannot and never will be able to be "good" enough to deserve to go to heaven. We cannot earn salvation. We cannot earn our way into a right relationship with God. How long have you ever kept a New Year's resolution? What about trying to quit smoking? How are you doing with the commandment concerning coveting?

Let me give you one of my favorite examples of our preoccupation with self. It is an example that Dr. Mollegen, one of my professors at seminary, used. It is an example of how our original sin can take something good and ruin it. Not only can—but often does. Let's imagine a little fantasy. Let us say that you decide to tithe. Do you know what tithing is? You may not—at least, many Christians act as if they have never heard of it. Anyway, let's say that you decide to give God—through the church, the United Fund, charity, and ever so many ways—10 percent of everything you have, and everything you will get in the future. How long do you think it will be before you let other people know about it? I remember the first time my wife and I decided to tithe (see, I'm bringing this to your attention right now). When we first decided to tithe, it happened to be at a time when I was making the most money I had ever made. We were so pleased with our-

29

selves and what we were doing for God. You would be amazed at how I could work it into any conversation. At the slightest opportunity I would say something like, "Wouldn't it be nice if everyone tithed?" Actually, tithing is a wonderful thing—something we are supposed to do—otherwise we are stealing from God; but if we are not careful we ruin it by using it to build ourselves up in other people's eyes. Now, let's take this just a bit farther. Suppose you did begin tithing and never told anyone. Think how good you would feel. Not only did you give God 10 percent of all you had and intend to give him 10 percent of all you get in the future, but you didn't tell a living soul. How good you are just makes you warm all over. It almost makes you burst with thinking about how wonderful, religious, and committed you are. In either case, concern with self is uppermost in our minds.

No! If I am ever going to make it, I've got to have a saviour. If I am ever going to have a meaningful relationship with God, and with my fellowman, then I've got to have a saviour—and Praise God, I have one! Having the right relationship with God and with my fellowman is what salvation is, but because of my self-preoccupation, my inclination to assert myself over everyone else—including God—I separate myself from him and my fellowman. When I exalt myself and make me number one, then God isn't number one with me. There can be only one number one. There can be only one center. If I put me in the center, God and I are separated—and I do the separating. God doesn't get mad and go off and pout. I am the one that runs away from him. Several times recently I have read the statement, "If God seems far off, guess who moved?"

This is exactly the situation. You remember in the story of Adam and Eve after they had decided not to be obedient and to "play God," the story says that God went walking in the cool of the evening, and Adam hid himself. This is what man always does, after declaring his independence from God. It is the way we do when we have wronged another person. If we see him coming, we walk on the other side of the street, or even go around the block, in order to avoid meeting him and facing him. This is what we do to God. We avoid him; we separate ourselves from him. The bad thing is that I can't, and won't, do anything to change the situation. If it is to be changed, God will have to be the one who does something.

There is one statement in The Sermon on the Mount that really describes man's predicament. Jesus said, "Be ye perfect." Do you really understand what this means? It means: We flunk. *This is the bad news.* I can't be perfect. I can't keep God's Law. My complete self-centeredness prevents it. This is the bad news that so many people have never heard. So many of us are like that old cartoon that shows two people with their feet propped up on a desk, and the caption reads: "Tomorrow we've got to get organized." Many people feel that if they really buckled down—if they really made up their minds and disciplined themselves, they could do it. They have never heard the bad news of the impossibility of "keeping the Law." Man must have a savior, or he is lost. But, *no one ever accepts a savior until he realizes he needs one.* The impossibility of being "good" enough destroys my relationship with God and with my fellowman. It has always been this way. Man has always messed up, and he is helpless to change the situation—so, God himself did something about it. *This is the good news;* but until it finally dawns on us, each of us, that we cannot do it, no matter how hard we try, we are not ready, we are not able, we cannot hear the good news.

Chapter Two
GOD'S SOLUTION

God's solution to our problem is the Good News. I have divided it into three parts and put it in outline form. This is to try and make it as easily understood as I can. This clarifies it in my own mind and has been beneficial in my attempts to explain it to other people.

First: *The Cross brought Salvation*. This is a theological statement that says that the death of Jesus Christ restored me to the right relationship with God. My sins have been completely covered over; I am forgiven. The chasm caused by my disobedience and my rebellion against God has been bridged over, and he and I are no longer separated. There are many explanations of how this was possible, but the one that I like and understand best is the "courtroom experience." It is as if I stood before Christ the Judge, and he asks, "Did you keep the Law? Did you break any of the Ten Commandments? Have you always put God first in everything and loved your fellowman the same way you love yourself?" I reply, "Yes, I am afraid I have broken the Commandments—most of them anyway. I have not kept the Law. I have failed miserably at putting God ahead of everything and loving my fellowman the way I have always loved myself. But, I have been a pretty good fellow—much better than many." Christ the Judge then says, "Pretty good doesn't count. God demands perfection. I am required by Divine Law to sentence you to death." Immediately the Judge steps down from the bench; and he, himself, takes the penalty; and I am acquitted, though guilty.

I realize that this is an oversimplification, and it surely doesn't make sense, humanly speaking; but the Grace of God doesn't make sense. The Grace of God, the unmerited, undeserved favor and mercy of God toward rebellious, disobedient, self-centered man, never makes sense. Part of the Good News is that God doesn't play by man's rules. There on the cross, the mercy of God met the justice of God. It does not mean that God is just a kindly, indulgent person who lets man get away with anything, or everything. The cross shows that God's justice cannot ignore man's sin. Sin is a serious thing to God. The cross shows just how serious it is to him, but the nature of God is love. He is not indulgent, sentimental love. God cannot afford to say, "Oh well, it doesn't matter." The worst thing God could say to us is, "I don't care what you do." That would mean that he doesn't love us. This is true with human parents. The worst thing a human parent can tell his child is that he doesn't care what he does. It does matter to God, and Good Friday shows just how much it matters. On the cross our sins were forgiven, God's justice was satisfied, and we were restored to the right relationship with our Heavenly Father.

Second: *Jesus was the Example.* As I tried to explain in the chapter on The Bad News, we were born self-centered.

If nothing changes us, we remain this way our entire lives. This leads to death—sometimes physical death, but always spiritual death. There is no room in our hearts and in our lives for anyone else—including God. The people we love are people we need in order to make, and keep, us happy. Scripture says that the wages of sin is death. We receive spiritual death as the result of a completely self-centered life. This death takes place long before physical death. This obsession with self separates us from God, and from our fellowman. The most completely self-centered man I ever knew was also one of the wealthiest. The townspeople didn't like him, and I don't believe his family did either. Although he thought only of himself, I do not believe that he liked himself. He was a miserable man. He was dead years before he finally stopped breathing. This is the natural and inevitable consequence and fate of everyone, if something doesn't change man's human nature. Jesus offered an alternative.

Jesus taught that if we put God at the center of our lives, this too will lead to death—death to self-obsession and worship; but out of this death comes the resurrection life. This resurrection life takes place here on earth—and continues after physical death. This is not only what he taught, but what he lived out. He didn't want to die on the cross. He prayed in the Garden of Gethsemane that if there could be any other way he would like to be spared, but nevertheless, "Thy will be done." He put God's will first. He died to self, and it cost him his physical life; but out of his self-offering, his dying to self, in obedience to his Father's will, came the Resurrection. He lived out his earlier statement that "He who would save his life will lose it, but he who

35

loses his life for my sake will gain it." He lost his life for God's sake, but gained eternal life for himself, and for those who are baptized into him.

In spite of this wonderful example, something more is needed. A lived-out example is really not too much help. Oh, I know that it gives us something to shoot for, but it really doesn't help us much. If you take a little six-year-old boy and a five-year-old girl you will usually find that small girls often learn quicker and are better coordinated. If you say, "Johnny, Susie can tie her shoes. Why can't you?" you are merely pinpointing a problem. The fact that Susie can tie her shoes and will be glad to show Johnny how well she can doesn't help him to be able to tie his. It only makes him dislike Susie. It doesn't help me one bit for you to say, "I know someone who lost forty pounds, why don't you?" I don't like you for telling me, nor him for doing it. I need more than an example. I need some power to help me do what I cannot do on my own.

Jesus told us the way to stay in the right relationship with God. He told us how we could enjoy living life the way it was meant to be lived. It means putting God at the center of our lives—listening to him and obeying him . . . trusting him and his love for us. In Jesus' life, and in his death, he acted out this principle.

By his death my sins were forgiven, and the relationship with God was restored, but there has to be more. If there is not, then the same thing that caused the separation before will cause it again. I need some power to aid me. I need something that will give me a new nature, a new spirit, a new power, a new kind of life. This is what happened on Pentecost. This is the last part of the Good News.

Third: *God sent his Holy Spirit to give man the power to do and be what God originally intended man to do and be.* Through this Gift, he has provided the direction and the power—the means whereby we can begin to live eternal life NOW. I grew up thinking that Christianity only meant "pie in the sky bye and bye when you die." Christianity is NOW religion which continues forever. This gift of the Holy Spirit is the "down payment" on the full inheritance one day, but this "first fruits" of the full inheritance is to help us begin living eternal life on earth. Here on earth we are intended to live the abundant life in a relationship of love with God and with our fellowman. This gift at Pentecost is the Third Person of the Trinity; and he transforms us, and our lives, if we cooperate and allow him to do so. We receive a new nature—God-centered rather than self-centered. We receive new goals and purposes—the goals and purposes of God. We begin to live a new life, a new kind of life, because God has provided the direction and the power for it.

The original Disciples were no special people before Jesus chose them. They were much like you and me: weak, sinful, self-centered men, until they were radically changed by the coming of the Holy Spirit on Pentecost. We have seen so many paintings of the Disciples that there is a tendency to assume that they walked around with halos floating some six inches above their heads, and people could spot them coming from the glow of those halos. People also assume that the Disciples knew and understood the whole situation and were merely walking through their roles in Jesus' plan. Jesus himself didn't know the whole detailed plan. When he came on earth he limited himself to the person of a first-century Jew. He knew nothing about

37

atomic energy and other scientific facts. He, like others of his generation, thought the world was flat. Jesus was not God "playing like he was a man." He was fully man, and limited. In the Incarnation, he had a deeper understanding of God and his own fellowman, but in the Incarnation it was necessary that he operate in the world as man. His Power came as a result of his perfect surrender and obedience to his Heavenly Father, and his complete saturation by the Holy Spirit. In perfect obedience and reliance upon God, he lived one day at a time, daily seeking divine guidance. This is why it was necessary for him to spend so much time in prayer. It was absolutely necessary that he stay in constant contact with the Father.

It was not until after the Resurrection and the coming of the Holy Spirit that the Disciples really understood who Jesus was and what he had been talking about while he was with them in the flesh. During the two or three years that he lived with them, they thought he was planning to establish a political kingdom, much as it had been in King David's time. Two of them were jockeying for the position of secretary of state. All of them deserted him, one of them betrayed him, and Peter denied him three times. It was not until *after* Pentecost that they really understood what he had been talking about. It was not until after the coming of the Holy Spirit that they were changed into new people, cowards into heroes, weaklings into strong men, followers into leaders.

If you have ever seen a mystery movie twice, the second time you see little things—little obvious things. Significant things happen that seemed insignificant the first time. Once you had seen the ending, everything was clear and seemed so obvious. It was like this for the Disciples after the Resurrection and the Pentecost event. Then they could say, "Now I understand what he was talking about, and what he meant." Now they could do what was impossible before. They understood the point of his death. They understood the purpose of God's Plan for man and had the power and the guidance to carry out their part in it.

The Holy Spirit is the enabling power of God who will enable anyone to do anything that God calls him to do—by supplying the direction and the ability which would not otherwise be there. If he is allowed to take charge, if we are open to him, we become what God wills to make us. We find the power to change situations, to meet problems, and to live life to the fullest because we are reborn, brand new people. The Disciples were so changed that they were able to forget their fears as they committed their lives to this Lord they had come to know. They were able to love without being loved in return; they could love with no strings attached. They could forgive, because they knew themselves forgiven; they could accept all others, because they knew themselves accepted—and they knew that they did not deserve this love, forgiveness, and acceptance. They were able to do all this in the power of the Holy Spirit. They found the peace of God. They claimed, and used, the gifts he gave. As they obediently followed the guidance of the Holy Spirit, they found that they could live this new kind of life and carry on the ministry that Jesus had commissioned them to do. They found that they could perform miracles in his name. They were able to carry on his mission and ministry as he had told them to do. They realized that there is no business like God's business. This same power, mission, and ministry has been passed on to everyone who commits his life to Jesus Christ. The third part of the Good News is the gift of this power from God to do and be what is otherwise impossible with our human nature and abilities. It becomes the norm of life under the power of God, the Holy Spirit.

Chapter Three
YOU'VE GOTTA BE KIDDING

On the first night of one of my Teaching Missions the dialogue goes something like this:

I ask, "Do you believe everything I have said?" A few hands go up, or a few heads nod up and down, but one can tell that the majority seem more confused than anything else because I have presented something that seems to go counter to what many of them have put together as their "theology." Most people sort of pick and choose just what parts of the Bible they will concern themselves with; and much of the time their theology is a mosaic of bits and pieces from various denominations, plus their own interpretations. If we are not careful, we bear down on the parts we like and skip over the parts we do not like. Many ministers are guilty of concentrating on certain pet themes, thereby ignoring other parts. So, I check them out. "I don't care, at this time, to get into a philosophical discussion about Heaven. I believe that Heaven begins here on earth; but just to see if you really accept what I have said, all of you who are going to Heaven, please hold up your hand. By Heaven I mean, all of you who will be, or will continue to be, with God when you die, hold up your hand." Generally speaking, two or three hold up their hands, but the majority do not. "Why did the rest of you not hold your hands up? You just got through saying you believe what I have said. Why didn't you put your hands up?"

There is a lot of hemming and hawing, or silence, for several minutes until finally someone says, "I'm not sure." "Why aren't you sure?" "I don't know whether or not I am good enough." That is what I have been waiting for. "You aren't, and you never will be good enough to deserve to go to Heaven; but what has that got to do with it?" No matter what many Christians profess, deep down they believe that they are going to have to "earn" their salvation. Although they readily mouth the words "salvation by grace" they really mean "salvation by works."

To try to show them that this is straight Christianity that I am teaching, I get out my Revised Standard Version of the Bible and turn to the Epistle to the Romans. "How many of you have read Romans? How many of you have studied Romans?" Usually there are several hands raised. "Did you hold up your hands when I asked how many were going to Heaven?" Most of them say, "No." "Then evidently, you have not understood what you have read or studied, because through and through the letter to the Romans is the dominant theme: salvation by grace, alone."

That theme is stated in the sixteenth and seventeenth verses of chapter one of the epistle: "For I am not ashamed of the gospel: it is the power of God for salvation to everyone who has faith, to the Jew first, and also to the Greek. For in it the righteousness of God is revealed through faith for faith; as it is written, 'He who through faith is righteous shall live.'" THIS MEANS "NO WORKS" FOR SALVATION.

Romans 3:20-28 says it plainly: "For no human being will be justified in his sight by works of the law. For we hold that a man is justified by faith apart from works of law."

Over and over it says the same thing in such passages as 4:1-8, 4:13-16, 5:1, 5:9, and 6:23. From beginning to end: NO WORKS *to gain salvation.*

Little girls can enter the Girl Scout program at the age of seven as Brownies, and they work their way up by earning Brownie points. My two daughters went through this, and my wife received a ten-year pin in working with the Scouting program. Anyone who has been a Brownie, or worked with them, will know what I mean when I say that you can sum up the Epistle to the Romans in three words: "No Brownie points." This same thing is stated in some other Epistles, such as the Epistle to the Galatians.

Once when I was doing this for a group, someone said, "Well, that is just Paul talking." Apparently he wanted it written in red ink from the lips of Jesus himself. My wife went to work so that we could go to the Head Man to prove this "new" theology—it is only about two thousand years old; but people often ask me where I got this new idea. This in itself shows how uninformed many people are concerning the Christian faith. Anyway, my wife found one example of what we needed in the Gospel according to St. John (6:27-29): Jesus said, " 'Do not labor for the food which perishes, but for the food which endures to eternal life, which the Son of man will give you; for on him has God the Father set His seal!' Then they said to him, 'What must we do, to be doing the works of God?' Jesus answered them, 'This is the work of God, that you believe in him

43

whom he has sent.' " *Nothing concerning earning points for good works.*

I agree that if one has faith, and truly believes in Jesus, it will show up in his life and his deeds, but salvation is a gift, not a reward. If anyone asks you, "Are you saved?" as a Christian you should say, "Yes." And, if they want to know when you were saved—meaning date and hour—you can say, "Friday before the first Easter—around three o'clock in the afternoon."

There is a familiar story that I use that seems to make this point with many people. I think that it tells the whole meaning of the Good News.

It seems that there was an Episcopalian who died and reached the Pearly Gates. St. Peter met him and said, "It takes a thousand points to get in; and I don't know you, so tell me something about yourself." The man said "Well, until I was twenty-one years old I never missed Sunday school unless I was sick in bed. I have a string of perfect attendance medals that almost reaches to the floor. I was an acolyte, active in the youth group, and I often worked around the church cutting grass, etc." St. Peter said, "That is extremely good. That gives you one point. Tell me something else about yourself." The man said, "Well I am seventy years old. I attended church regularly, served on the vestry many times, sang in the choir, and was a lay reader. I always tithed and was a lifelong Episcopalian." St. Peter said, "This is truly remarkable. That gives you another point. Tell me something else about yourself." The man said, "I tried to live the Christian life. I lived by the Golden Rule, do not believe I had an enemy in the world, and was truly concerned—in word and deed—about the welfare of my fellowman." St. Peter said, "This is truly wonderful. That is another point. Tell me something else about yourself." By this time the man was getting a little irritated, and said, "At this rate, the only way I'll get into Heaven is by the grace of God." St. Peter said, "That is one thousand points, and with the three you earned it makes one thousand and three. Would you like to come in?"

A lifetime of good works, and it earned him three points. This story merely illustrates the impossibility of *earning* salvation. Quite often, people resent this and say, "Well then, you mean that we can do anything we want to and still go to Heaven?" Even this question has as its basis the deeply instilled idea that salvation is the reward for "being good" and "giving up" doing what we want to do. We are called on to live as befits an adopted child of God, out of gratitude and love. If we could only learn that "being good" should be the result of salvation—and it is not the cause of salvation. To try and illustrate this, I use an example I once heard Bishop George Murray use:

Let's say that a man is cheating on his wife, and she finds out about it. He says, "Oh, oh, I'm going to buy her some flowers and candy and go to her and beg her to forgive me." But before he can, his wife comes to him and says, "I love you, and I forgive you." *Now* he buys her some candy and flowers—and perhaps a fur coat—not to obtain her forgiveness, but out of grateful penitence. If he had given her the presents first, he would have been trying to buy her forgiveness. That is what many people are trying to do to God. They are trying to buy forgiveness and salvation with "good works" instead of living out a love relationship with God out of grateful penitence.

I know a man who is a living example of the man who met St. Peter at the Pearly Gates. His life was spent "being good" and "doing good." He was not pretending; he really was a good man. When he first heard my Teaching Mission it almost made him sick when I told him his "goodness" meant nothing as far as affecting his relationship with God toward salvation. Although he was a kind man by nature, and a dedicated Christian and churchman, deep down he felt that this was having some influence on his qualification for Heaven. For a short while he was a disturbed man—especially since I was his new minister—but a little later on the real good news sank home to him, and he now does more than he ever did before—if that is possible; but he does it for a different reason. He does it cheerfully, gladly, and extremely competently. This man is one of the greatest examples of a happy Christian that I have ever known. He spends his life in the service of Jesus Christ—and he does it joyfully. His joy is in allowing Jesus Christ to be his Lord, and not in trying to run his life on his own terms. He knows he needs a saviour. He has found one in Jesus Christ, and is willing for him to rule his life.

Chapter Four

THE ABUNDANT LIFE

With the coming of the Holy Spirit, the Disciples began living the abundant life. This by no means implies that they no longer had any problems. Indeed, they took on many problems because they were followers of Jesus Christ— problems they could have avoided if they had been willing to deny Jesus Christ as their Lord. Some of the original Disciples were killed, many of the early followers died as martyrs for Christ, and material blessings were few. Because they were filled with the Spirit and the love of Christ, they shared with each other that which they did have. The abundant life they lived was because of the power they possessed, and were possessed by. They knew themselves loved, forgiven, and accepted by God and were able to offer these same things to other people. They had the peace of God which gave them confidence that whether they lived or died they were in God's hands. Their hearts were set on eternal life with God as they lived in the kingdom of God on earth.

Many Christians spend their lives waiting for some emotional "charge" complete with an unmistakable surge of power and an undeniable message from God before they move out of the category of nominal church members. What they fail to realize is that they have been given everything that the Disciples were given—the power AND the commission from Christ. Luke 24:46-49 is an account of Jesus' charge to the Disciples: " 'Thus it is written, that the Christ should suffer and on the third day rise from the dead, and that repentance and forgiveness of sins should be preached in his name to all nations, beginning from Jerusalem. You are witnesses of these things. And behold, I send the promise of my Father upon you; but stay in the city, until you are clothed with power from on high.' "

Acts 1:3-8 reaffirms this charge:

To them he presented himself alive after his passion by many proofs, appearing to them during forty days, and speaking of the kingdom of God. And while staying with them he charged them not to depart from Jerusalem, but to wait for the promise of the Father, which, he said, "you heard from me, for John baptized with water, but before many days you shall be baptized with the Holy Spirit!" So when they had come together, they asked him, "Lord, will you at this time restore the kingdom to Israel?" He said to them, "It is not for you to know times or seasons which the Father has fixed by his own authority. But you shall receive power when the Holy Spirit has come upon you; and you shall be my witnesses in Jerusalem and in all Judea and Samaria and to the end of the earth."

The Church is the successor to the original Disciples, and the same charge is laid on it that was laid on them. All Christians have received the power and the charge from Christ. They already have all they are going to get—but the majority have not claimed it and acted upon it, and therefore they remain pretty much in-name-only Christians who feel that somehow or other something is missing. The only thing missing is the tangible results that should follow the gift and the charge from Jesus Christ. It corresponds to the idea of someone depositing a certain amount of money in the bank in your name, telling you the money is there, and asking you to use it for a designated purpose. If you never draw out any of it and use it the way it was intended, it might as well not be there.

At baptism, or whenever we accept Jesus Christ as our Lord and saviour, he deposits his gift and issues his charge to us. If we never draw upon his gift, it might as well not be there. If Christians only realized that they have been chosen, called, given a task, and equipped to fulfill that task, the church would be as dynamic and *on fire* today as it was in the first century A.D.; and Christians would have accomplished more than they have in bringing the world under the Lordship of Jesus Christ.

God never gives us a task without also giving us the power to perform it. How and when do we receive this power? In the Episcopal Church we emphasize the sacraments as "special points of contact with God" through which we receive this power.

The initial gift is given at our baptism; shifts into high gear at Confirmation when we accept or renew our pledge of allegiance to Jesus Christ as Lord as well as saviour; and this power is constantly maintained by the other sacraments, private prayer and Bible study, along with corporate worship in the fellowship of other Christians.

Through these things Jesus provides a way that we can experience his presence and power, NOW. Through them,

the very strength, love, courage, guidance, and power of
Christ himself is conveyed to his followers. He promised to
send his Spirit to be with his followers. He promised to
send his power and told them that "he who believes in me
will also do the works that I do; and greater works than
these will he do, because I go to the Father" (John 14:12).
If we do not believe, claim, and act on his promise, there is
a twofold loss: we deny ourselves of his gifts and presence;
and the ministry and mission of Jesus Christ to the world
is greatly diminished.

The original Disciples found that they could love in a
new way—completely different from the natural, human,
self-centered way. This new kind of love is called AGAPE.
It means being able to love with no strings attached, no
provisions, and no qualifications. Human love says, "I'll
love you if, or provided, you do such and such a thing."
Agape, Christian love, says, "I'll love you regardless." The
original Disciples found that they could love, forgive, and
accept because they found themselves loved, forgiven, and
accepted—and they knew they did not deserve it. They
were able to do this through this newly given power.

Saved by grace not only means that we are saved from
eternal separation from God—it also means that we can
live in the constant presence of God. We are not only saved
from something, but are saved *for* something. We are saved
in order that we may live this abundant life of love, forgiveness, and acceptance ourselves, and offer it to everyone
we come into contact with. In this abundant life, the Christian receives the peace of God, the presence of Christ, and
the power of the Holy Spirit. This truly becomes "Good
News" to people who have been living lives of frustration,

anxiety, defeat, and hostility. They come to know in a personal way what is meant by Christian joy. This is a large part of what all the shouting is about. It means that Christ has given us the ability to live without hating, envying, and climbing over one another in order to "get ahead." It means being out from under the crushing burden of guilt and inferiority complexes. Our guilt was covered over on the cross, and how dare we feel inferior when Christ thought enough of us to die for us?

Like so many people of my generation, I grew up with the idea that everything about Christianity was "in the sweet bye and bye"; and if I could just get through life without displeasing God too much, he might let me enjoy Heaven one day. What I did not hear, or what was not said, was the fact that Heaven, eternal life, and the abundant life are all the same—and they begin here on earth. This new kind of life which is *a right relationship with God which in turn produces a right relationship with our fellowman* is the real point of Christianity. The Good News includes the fact that Jesus Christ came to live and die that we might begin to live this eternal life now.

Christians are not perfect. We *shall* be one day, but God has all eternity to make us perfect. His job is to transform us; our job is to open ourselves to him and let him work his will in us. Since most of us keep reviving the "old" man who died at our baptism, we continue to let self try to replace God as the center of our lives. One of the glories of the Good News is that we can confess and receive forgiveness and call on the power we need to help us lead the abundant life, the power to BE what we are meant to be—obedient children of God. God forgives the penitent, and

51

will transform and use the person who is open to him and offers him obedience.

This is what the original Disciples discovered. They found that they could live this new kind of life in spite of persecution and hardships. They began eternal life then and there. They spread the Gospel by word and deed, brought others into the Christian fellowship, and saw Christianity begin to change the civilized world. The opportunity to live this kind of life, continue the ministry of Christ, and carry out his commission is offered to us. This new kind of life is what the world needs so desperately. Imagine the exhilarating feeling of knowing, and accepting, the fact that one is forgiven, loved, and accepted—*as he is*. Christ did not say, "I'll die for you when you get good enough." He died for us, and accepts us, as we are. He will change us if we will allow him to; but the change doesn't come first. The change is the result of salvation, not the cause of salvation. Imagine the relief of not having to put up a front in order to impress people, or erect barriers to keep them from really knowing you. Jesus said, "Ye shall know the Truth, and the Truth shall set you free." People are bound by the chains of self-centeredness. Real living is hampered by the pressures of society, and life is dissipated by the attempt to obtain the values of this world and meet its standards. In Jesus Christ we are freed from this. In him we find the power to live, rather than just exist. We have his word, "I came to bring you life, and that life more abundant."

Chapter Five
IS IT TRUE?

It concerns me greatly that, with all the millions of Christians in the world, so few of them enjoy this abundant life that Christ came to bring? Why are there so many unhappy, frustrated Christians living dull, unfulfilled lives? Why is so much of the Church made up of nominal, in-name-only Christians who seem to be merely *playing church* as they go through the motions without exhibiting the joy and power that Christianity promises? I believe that I know what it is that blocks people from enjoying these benefits. For purposes of clarity, I have divided the reason into three blocks, but actually, they are all three variations of the *one* block. I will deal with the first block in this chapter and the other two in chapters eight and nine.

The first is: MOST PEOPLE DO NOT TRUST GOD. People are afraid to take a chance on him. They believe that they will have to give up what is enjoyable if they truly offer their lives to God. I am convinced that we must be willing to give up anything, or everything, but that he seldom asks us to do so. Many businessmen believe that it is impossible to be successful and a *committed* Christian at the same time in this dog-eat-dog world. They honestly feel that they would lose their businesses, their families would suffer because other people would take advantage of them, and they just cannot afford to take the chance. What this really means is that they do not trust God. This is why their business has to come before God's business. This is the reason why many Christians do not tithe. The amount of money has nothing to do with it actually. They really believe that they could not pay their bills or they would seriously deprive their families of needed things if they were to give God back 10 percent of the 100 percent that he has given them. Not only does this mean that they do not trust God —it also means that they do not believe that he gave them the 100 percent; nor do they believe that they owe him 10 percent.

Because they do not trust God, they either close their eyes to the fact that he has given them what they have or they are willing to steal from him. When we refuse to tithe, we *are* stealing from God. Some people will not allow themselves to face this fact, and so they rationalize about what they return to God. Refusing to face a fact does not change a fact. I have never known a person who tithed who did not find that he got back more than the 10 percent he returned to God; but many people are afraid to trust him, to put him to the test, to see how the Lord works. We read from the prophet Malachi (3:7-10):

From the days of your fathers you have turned aside from my statutes and have not kept them. Return to me, and I will return to you, says the Lord of Hosts. But you say, "How shall we return?" Will man rob God? Yet you are robbing me. But you say, "How are we robbing thee?" In your tithes and offerings. You are cursed with a curse, for you are robbing me; the whole nation of you. Bring the full tithes into the storehouse, that there may be food in my house; and thereby put me to the test, says the Lord of Hosts, if I will not open the windows of heaven for you and pour down for you an overflowing blessing.

Many people who would never think about going back on a promise they had made to a friend, or even to an acquaintance, think nothing about going back on vows they have made to God. Their baptism and/or confirmation vows mean nothing to them. Many people who would never think of stealing from another person, think nothing of stealing from God. The prophet Malachi was dealing with the same sort of people in his day. He was alarmed at the way people cheated God. They, as was the religious custom of the day, offered sacrifices to God, but some of them offered blemished sacrifices, instead of their best. Many Christians today merely "tip" God and offer him the "left-overs" of their lives. They offer God something of what is left-over after all their personal needs and desires are taken care of. I believe that God is speaking to us today through the words of the prophet Malachi, particularly in 1:6-8 and 1:13-14 where he condemns the people for offering unfit sacrifices to God and tells them to try it on their human ruler and see what happens. He also berates them for complaining that it is too difficult to serve God and do what he asks. He says that God declares "Cursed is the man who promises a fine ram from his flock and substitutes a sick one to sacrifice to God." This certainly seems to apply to the person who professes Jesus Christ as Lord as well as Saviour, but then refuses to serve and follow him.

God asks us to test him. We are not supposed to tempt him. This is what Jesus refused to do when he was tempted by the devil, but God welcomes our testing of him to see whether or not he is faithful to his promises. The reason we cheat God, and will not tithe him our money, time, and talent, is that we do not trust him.

Many people are afraid to get serious about Jesus Christ. Many teen-agers are afraid that their friends will shun them, that they will have to be "goody-goodies" or do-gooders if they become anything more than nominal church-going Christians. Most of them seem to feel that that is something they can do after they get much older. I remember one of the songs from the stage play and movie, *Bye Bye Birdie*. It was entitled, "I've got a Lot of Living to Do." So many teen-agers are afraid that committing their lives to Jesus Christ will hamper that lot of living they've got to do. If only they were willing to take a chance on God and find out that what he offers enhances living—it does not hamper it.

It seems almost inevitable that when people are giving some thought to getting serious about their Christian faith, they rack their brains trying to figure out what they would hate to do the most, and then decide that that is what God will want them to do. If it is a man, he immediately thinks he will have to quit his job and go to seminary. He thinks about having to give up his standard of living, all the luxuries, most of the pleasures, and become a *preacher*. If it is a woman, she figures she has got to go to Africa and be a missionary. I actually had one woman stand up at one of my Missions and almost shout that she didn't want to leave her husband and children and go to Africa as a missionary. God hadn't mentioned the idea to her. She just decided that this is what would happen; so she could not, or would not, offer herself to him. Somewhere along the line, a great many people have forgotten that God is love and that he wants only the best for us. This is why they refuse to trust him. We sing the hymn "What a Friend We Have in Jesus" meaning that we hope he will help us when we need him. But if we really think he is our friend, why won't we trust him? When we love someone, we want the best for him. We love ourselves although we may not like ourselves at times, and we want the best for ourselves . . . AND THAT IS EXACTLY WHAT GOD WANTS FOR US. He loves us enough to have sent his Son to die for us so that we would not be separated from him; he loves us so much that he sent his Son to give us the abundant life, the Holy Spirit with all his gifts; and yet, when it comes to letting him continue to give us the good things of life, we are afraid to trust him. This lack of trust in a God we *say* is love is one of the reasons we are blocked from enjoying the abundant life Christ has promised and provided.

Part of this feeling of distrust is a holdover from some people and some denominations who intentionally or unintentionally imply that Jesus said, "I came to bring you the more restricted life," instead of "I came to bring you the more abundant life." I grew up believing that Christianity insisted that if it is fun, it must be sinful. The emphasis seem to be, "Be good, and you will go to Heaven; be bad, and you will go to hell." To many people, *being good* means not enjoying one's self, and *being bad* means having fun. Hellfire and damnation preaching was an attempt to scare people out of hell and into Heaven. This just doesn't work. If people were only taught to believe the Christian truth that God wants our love, not our fear, they would be more inclined to trust him and respond to his love. You cannot scare anyone into loving God anymore than you can scare your own children into loving you. If you say to them, "Love me or I'll beat your head in," they may become frightened of you, but it will not make them love you.

Being AFRAID of God, and FEARING him are not the same thing. To fear him is to hold him in awe, reverence, and respect. He wants this from us, and it is exactly what we should offer him, but how could a God who is love want us to be afraid of him? Since people cannot be scared into loving God or into being good, many rebel and drift away —or run away—from the Church. Even so, our whole society in this so-called enlightened age is still subconsciously affected by the Puritan outlook, the Victorian Age, the Blue law principle, and the idea of earning one's way to Heaven. It is still difficult to accept the fact that since God is love he wants to give us only the best. Too many people seem to go along with the central character in the TV show *Maude* when she says, "God'll get you for that."

Chapter Six

TOO GOOD TO BE TRUE

We tend to think that the Pharisees were people who only lived back in the time of Jesus. The Christian church is loaded with Pharisees. These are the legalists, the ones who keep trying to earn salvation and who also insist that you keep the law. They forget—or never knew—that to love is to keep the Law of God. The first four Commandments speak of loving God and the last six speak of loving our fellowman. Jesus was sympathetic and concerned with the sinners, but he had little good to say for the Pharisees. They were out to get him because he spoke against their legalism. They were concerned with the letter of the law, while he was interested in the spirit of the law, which is love.

Our whole culture is slanted toward the concept of earning our way. We tell small children that we will buy them a toy if they are good. We tell school children that we will give them a dollar for every "A" they make on their school report cards, and we imply to them that we will not love them if they do not come up to certain standards we have adopted. Naturally, when it comes to religion, we think that it means that we have to earn our salvation. We seem to think that we must buy a ticket to Heaven with the points we have earned by doing certain things and by refraining from doing certain other things. Where is there any "good news" in that? What do people really mean when they say Jesus Christ is their Saviour, if they feel that they must save themselves by being good?

The Pharisees concentrated on Heaven as a reward instead of just responding in gratitude and love to the God who had already proven his love for them. There still existed in their minds something of the idea of appeasement of a wrathful God. Many present-day Christian "Pharisees" have never moved over into the New Testament. They are still people under the law. To them, status with God comes through human effort, not through the sacrificial death of Jesus Christ. Where is there any good news connected with a law I cannot keep? This is why some people get discouraged and just give up. They reject what they *think* is Christianity. In their case, they KNOW the bad news but have not HEARD the good news.

Many of the people who visited the nightclubs where I used to work were products of this kind of distorted, or incomplete, Christianity. It didn't stop them from drinking. It didn't stop them from dancing. It really did not do much of anything except make them feel guilty—and defensive. The "Heavenly Scoreboard" still looms large in many people's conception of God and his relationship to them. If only people would realize that being good—whatever that means—is a by-product of salvation and not the cause of salvation. We may be good because we have been saved, but we are not saved because we are good.

Some people actually resist the idea of salvation as a gift, and not as a reward. Sometimes there is actual hostility. I have seen people at my Teaching Missions look depressed when I show them scriptural proof. I have come to the conclusion that some people do not like to hear this, for three reasons:

First, *Many Christian church members have never gotten out of the old covenant of law and into Christ's covenant of grace.* The idea of change is painful; and some lifelong, but impossible ideas are more comfortable even when they present difficulty. Their faith is so shaky that they fear that anything that is new to them will completely crumble what faith they have. So, they would rather accept things on "faith" than think them out, with the possibility of admitting the necessity for a different way of thinking and acting.

Second, *it assaults man's pride.* We do not like to admit that we can't do anything. We kid ourselves, telling ourselves, that one day we will get around to keeping God's law. It hurts a prideful person to say, "God, I can't do it." As I have said before, "No one ever accepts a saviour until he knows he needs one. And, if you can do it then you don't need Jesus. Therefore, Jesus wasted his time and his life, as far as you are concerned.

Third, *it sounds too good to be true—too easy.* People insist that there must be a catch to it, that there must be something that we have to do other than put our faith in Jesus Christ. They say, "You never get anything for nothing." Jesus said, "Except ye become as little children, ye cannot enter the Kingdom of Heaven." When you offer a small child some candy, he doesn't question your motive or try to figure out whether or not he deserves it—HE JUST TAKES IT. That is exactly how we are to accept salvation through Jesus Christ. Of course, this does not mean that we do nothing—and later on I will speak about what our part is: but for now, let me put it this way: On the Cross, Jesus Christ bought my ticket to salvation. It cost me nothing. I did nothing for it, and yet, the ticket has my name on it. The only thing I have to do is pick up the ticket and get on the bus.

Good works are the response to the knowledge that one has been saved from separation from God; they are the natural consequences of realizing that God is love, and just how much he loves us. They seem to evolve out of the almost unbelieveable fact that if there had been only one person on earth, and you had been that person—Jesus Christ would still have died for you. Our life as Christians is the result of forgiveness, not the means to secure forgiveness. Christian ethics is grateful penitence. Of course, a great many nominal Christians are ingrates, and that is why they are nominal Christians.

If people trusted God, they would find that Christianity means the full, happy, exciting life—not necessarily the easy life, but so much greater than any other kind of life. It is not so much a "giving up" as a "filling out." I believe that my life is an example of this. People are either "kicked into Heaven" or "kissed into it." Praise God, I was kissed into it. I wish that more people would allow themselves to be kissed into it, instead of self-centeredly ignoring God, or actively rebelling against him, until something—a tragedy, or some turn of events—comes along and kicks them, out of desperation, into a dependence upon him which brings them into the right relationship with him. God wants to kiss us all into the right relationship with himself.

I have heard preachers tell about what terrible sinners they had been, what a life of degradation they had lived until they "found" Jesus. I do not doubt that this was true, but it was not this way for me. Before I ever got serious about my professed faith, I had a good life. I had a beautiful wife, five beautiful children, and good friends. I only worked three hours a night, at most, entertaining; did a couple of TV shows a day; cut some records now and then; and made more money than I will ever make again. I was well paid for doing a kind of work that was satisfying. I used to love to dance, go to parties, and play piano and sing. I had a great life. Many people who were products of the distorted Christianity I spoke of earlier didn't understand how I could serve on the vestry of my church, teach Sunday school with my wife, and still work in one of those "dens of iniquity," those sinful nightclubs. Nevertheless, I lived a happy, rewarding life. I knew that I was a sinner, but a forgiven one. I knew that whatever talent I had was God-given, and everything I had was from God. After I became serious about the vows that I had made to God at my baptism and confirmation, I still had a beautiful wife, five beautiful children, and I still enjoyed dancing, attending parties, and playing piano and singing—but my life was so much fuller, so much more exciting than it had been that there was really no comparison. I am living a great deal of the abundant life now. It would be even greater if I would allow the Holy Spirit to completely rule my life. The Christian life is one of joy and fulfillment. It certainly is not one that is joyless with a "holier than thou" attitude. What a terrible misrepresentation of the life Jesus came to bring is seen in the joyless, judgmental religion that some professing Christians live. The Christian life of joy and fulfillment is blocked by so many people because they do not trust God and his plan for them. They are afraid to take a chance on him; and so, for them, Christianity seems ineffective and distasteful.

Because they are afraid that they will have to give up more than they are willing to; they renege on the vows they have made to God and cheat themselves out of enjoying the abundant life he wants them to have. It has come to my attention how often I use examples dealing with food to illustrate my points, but I honestly believe that the abundant life is like moving up from hamburger to steak and lobster . . . from gelatin to cheesecake. The abundant life is like having humdrum, everyday life raised to the nth degree— to the highest power. It is having life raised to the highest power—God's power, the Spirit-filled life.

Chapter Seven
JESUS AS BOSS

Other than "God is love," I imagine that the most common statement in any Christian church is the vow that each Christian has made to God: "I accept Jesus Christ as my Lord and Saviour." I feel that this is so glibly said at baptism and/or confirmation that what is being said is completely missed. It is said, but not understood, by many of those who say it. Many never understand that this is a vow made to Almighty God—a vow that he expects them to keep. The real meaning of these two words, Lord and Saviour, is lost or misunderstood; and they seem to become only a stock phrase said by rote—the same way that the Lord's Prayer is often said without much thought to its real meaning and what is being said to God. So many Christians do not realize what they are actually saying to God when they pray the Lord's Prayer; and if they did, some would not pray it. They would be horrified if they realized that they were asking that his Kingdom come right now— regardless of what it would do to their comfortable, complacent life. They might not pray it if they understood that they were requesting that his will be done, no matter what the result might be. They might also be troubled if they realized that they were asking him to forgive them THE SAME WAY THAT THEY FORGAVE OTHERS. The Lord's Prayer is so powerful, but so misunderstood by so many people. The same sort of thing is true of the vow to accept Jesus as Lord and Saviour.

First, let's take the word SAVIOUR. This word has taken on the meaning of Jesus Christ exclusively, but I am talking about the word *saviour,* not capitalized. Obviously, when it is asked what this word means, the first answer is "someone who saves," and then such things as deliverer, helper, and the like. But I believe that it may help if we understand that saviour means: ANYONE, OR ANYTHING, THAT GIVES THE NUMBER ONE MEANING TO MY LIFE IS WHAT, OR WHOM, I HAVE MADE MY SAVIOUR. For millions of people this is Jesus Christ, but for millions of others—including many who profess Jesus to be their saviour—this can be alcohol, sex, food, job, status, money, health, or any number of things. There are many things that give meaning to a person's life, but whatever gives THE NUMBER ONE meaning is what he has made his saviour.

I think of movie actresses whose faces and figures are their saviours; and once they age a little and start losing their figures and lines begin to appear in their faces, they find themselves being offered fewer and smaller roles. Quite often, they take an overdose of sleeping pills—because their saviour has let them down. Or take the man whose job is so important to him that he neglects his wife, children, church, and everything else. Then comes the day when he is forced into retirement. It is not unusual when this has been the case to find that the man is dead within a year or less. He had depended upon a false saviour and served a false lord. In his case, his saviour let him down.

One example that is particularly vivid to me is the situation where a person has made his family his saviour. My mother did this to a large degree. Her family seemed to mean everything to her. She lived for it, and to serve it, almost to the exclusion of everything else. She was a willing slave to her family. I am sure that she loved my father, but the center of her life was her three sons. She didn't belong to any clubs or organizations—except the PTA, but even this was for us. She had few close friends because she really didn't have time for anything that interferred with her devotion to her children. It seems now, on looking back, that she lived vicariously through her children. Her joy and her sorrows came from our triumphs and joys and our day to day problems, misfortunes or defeats.

My oldest brother was what is called a hemophiliac, and he spent much of his life in pain. She nursed him and worried about him almost constantly. When he was twenty-nine years old, he died—and she died also. Oh, she existed for six more years, but she really died when he did. You see, her saviour let her down. Most of her reason for living was gone. As the youngest of the three children, I can honestly say that I do not remember ever feeling neglected or unloved to the slightest degree. I cannot speak for my older brother, the middle son. He was an unhappy person for most of his life, but I believe that this was due to something inside himself. Whatever feelings of inadequacy, or of being unloved, that he may have had were not due to any real inadequacy or lack of love. Our parents were wonderful people who loved us dearly. They were Christians, although I am not sure how fully they understood the benefits and responsibilities of being Christian. I know they prayed—particularly in times of trouble. My mother read the Bible privately and to us; but her life revolved around her family. Our home was her real church; her family seemed to be her god; and she daily offered herself as a living sacrifice. We were what made life worth living—in a sense, her saviours; but as it is with everything else, except Jesus Christ, we let her down. Jesus Christ—the same yesterday, today, and tomorrow—is the only saviour who never lets a person down.

I often have people tell me, after the first or second night of my Teaching Mission, that they really want to come back for the rest of it, but they have something else they just have to do. These things are legitimate reasons, such as taking the children somewhere, watching them play little league baseball, or any number of things. They sincerely hate to miss it; but I always tell them that it is perfectly all right, and they should not apologize. All of us do what we want to do. We all do many things that we do not want to do; but if there is something that is important enough to us—we manage to do it if it is at all physically possible. We do whatever is most important to us. It may not *be* the most important thing, but it is to us.

My best friend is a man that I have run around with since we were twelve years old. When I was in show business, he handled my publicity. We ate lunch together two or three times a week until I moved to Nashville recently. We are closer than most brothers. I have spent about a fourth of my life waiting for him. He is one of those people who is never on time—I don't mean that he is always a few minutes late; I mean that he runs into hours with his late-ness. He keeps his wife, his children, his friends, and his business waiting—sometimes for two or three hours at a time. He has such a good personality that people always forgive him. My wife used to give dinner parties and tell him they were for 6:30, hoping that he would make it for the 7:30 it was scheduled for. He would still manage to be late. He goes to a Methodist church, and he is there nearly every Sunday. He is late for Sunday school, and then some-how between Sunday school and the worship service, he manages to be late for the worship service.

I have never known him to be on time—except, that he has never missed an Alabama football game since 1945. He has never missed the kickoff—he has never missed the warm-up. He has a reputation for being the Crimson Tide's number one fan. If he spent as much money and time on the work of the church, they would probably do feature stories about him in church magazines. His enthusiasm, cheerfulness, and great personality would be a wonderful witness to the joy of Christianity.

Now, I am not judging him. My wife, Anne, tells me that she never judges people—she only makes "Christian eval-uations." Well, my friend could tell me that Jesus Christ is the most important thing in his life; but it is my Christian evaluation that he is not. My friend may be an exaggerated case, but the lives of many who profess Jesus Christ as the most important thing in their lives correspond to my friend's life. Their saviours may be different, but there seems to be evidence that Jesus has real competition with them, also.

Every Christian has said, "I accept Jesus Christ as my personal saviour"—but have we all really done this? Is

69

Jesus Christ the one who gives the number one meaning to our lives? Were we merely mouthing words?

Now, for the word LORD. This word doesn't mean as much to us as it would to the English and some Europeans, because their histories are full of lords in the secular sense. When I ask people what the word lord means they usually say master, ruler, etc., but these are almost religious clichés. The word *lord* really means "boss." When we say "I accept Jesus Christ as my Lord," it is supposed to mean that we have accepted him and are allowing him to be "boss" of our lives—but have we really?

Although many people are enjoying the wonderful life that Jesus came to bring because they have accepted him as the boss of their lives and as the one who gives the number one meaning to them, I am afraid that a great many church members are merely kidding themselves. They are "playing church" as they go through the motions and mouth the words, while at the same time they renege on the vow that they have made to Almighty God. These are the people who make up the nominal, in-name-only-Christians who are not finding the promises of Jesus Christ a reality in their lives. This lack of trust in God, plus wanting to be their own saviour, proves to be a terrible block to their living the abundant life.

Chapter Eight
HE KIDS YOU NOT

The second reason so few Christians enjoy this abundant life is that many of them DO NOT BELIEVE THE PROMISES OF JESUS CHRIST. Jesus made many promises, but there is one that sums them all up, as far as I am concerned. If this one is not true, then I have no confidence in any of them. If it is true, then we have no excuse and are cheating ourselves out of the abundant life and cheating him out of our allegiance and commitment. Thank God, it is true. Many have found this out. Many are beginning to find this out.

Jesus said, "Seek ye first the Kingdom of God, and his righteousness, and all these things shall be added unto you." To paraphrase this, "If you will put God at the center of your life, EVERYTHING you need in order for you to enjoy the full, abundant, happy, exciting life will be given to you." All too few Christians really believe this. If they did, they would act upon it. If they would act on his promise they would find that he is trustworthy. God is always faithful to his covenants. Because this is so, it is just poor business, even from a selfish viewpoint, not to believe him. We will put money in stocks; we will put money and our sweat into businesses that may fail; we will put our trust in other people—sometimes weak people like ourselves; but we are afraid to put our trust, our money, our efforts, in the one we profess to be our Lord and Saviour. If we really trusted him and believed his promises, we would put God at the center of our lives and see whether or not that promised abundant life becomes a reality for us. This is what he wants for us. This is what he has provided for us, but we must step out on faith in him. Since so many people do not step out in faith, evidently they do not really believe him.

Our unbelief proves to be a giant block to our enjoyment of the wonderful life Jesus Christ came to give us. Belief is the door, unbelief is the block. Faith is stepping through that door to the abundant life that awaits us.

Chapter Nine

THY KINGDOM COME, MY WILL BE DONE

The third reason so few Christians enjoy the abundant life is that THEY DO NOT WANT GOD'S WILL DONE. Some people realize this and admit it, but many others do not. Every time we pray the Lord's Prayer we say, "Thy Kingdom come, thy will be done, on earth as it is in Heaven." We have prayed this prayer so often, and so carelessly, that many people do not know what they are actually saying. This phrase means that we want God's kingdom to come in right now, even though it will upset most of our situations, change our standards, and alter our lives. It also means that we want God's will done perfectly here on earth, in our lives, the way it is done perfectly in Heaven. I do not believe that the majority of people who pray this really mean this. Whenever I make this statement at one of my Missions, there are always a few who very adamantly say that they *do* want God's will done. I realize that there are some people who want God's will done—no matter what it may entail and what it may do to our complacent, self-centered way of living; but many people only think they want God's will done. Some of the people hedge and say, "Well, what is God's will?" What they mean is, "You tell me what God's will is, and I'll decide whether or not I will do it." This means they want to remain in charge;

they want to make the final decision and have veto power. It is much like the old saying that people want to serve God—but in an advisory capacity. The prayer means "Whatever your will is, Heavenly Father, I want it to be done; and I am willing to do whatever you want me to do." Many people who think they want God's will done ignore his stated will in the Bible. We know he wants us to love, forgive, and accept *everyone*—but we don't do it. What makes us think we will do other things that are his will, if they clash with what we want? Most of us want *our* will done and for God to put his stamp of approval on it.

To illustrate how we kid ourselves about this, let's consider another fantasy:

Let us say that one night there is a sudden knock at your door. It is a messenger with a celestial telegram from God. There is no doubt but that it is definitely from him, and it says, "I want you to integrate. I want you to intermarry. I want a worldwide malt-colored race." signed God. You can imagine how well this goes over in most of the churches in the South where I have done this. I remember one ultra-conservative church were I used this example. One dowager-type lady said, "God wouldn't do that to me." I replied, "I know, but what if he did?" and again she repeated, "He wouldn't do that to me." We went back and forth with our statements about four or five times, but she never gave an inch. She would not admit to the remotest possibility that God might want something that was distasteful to her to happen. I hadn't said that he did; I merely asked what would be their individual reaction *if* he did. I am sure that I lost her from then on. Her mind closed on my statement and never got the point that I was trying to make. I am afraid that most of us act on this same principle of refusing to admit the possibility of God wanting us to do something that we do not want to do. We decide what God wants, and it seldom is something that we feel strongly negative toward.

To try to dispel any fear that I might be a trouble-maker who was trying to spread this "communist" sort of thing, I mentioned that the race situation was not a topic for this three-night Mission. I was merely using the example in order to try to get their attention—and, you know, I think I did.

This same idea applies to Christian blacks. What if they got such a celestial telegram telling them that God wanted them to forgive completely all the injustices that have been committed against them? What about forgiving the slights, the discriminations, the hostilities they have endured? Are they willing to love and forgive the ones who have committed these injustices? Would the blacks be willing to do God's will, regardless? This is what he is asking them to do.

I use this example to try to show that we rationalize and skip over the parts of the Bible and the Christian religion that we do not agree with or are afraid of. This applies to many things. In my own case, if I got a celestial telegram from God saying that he wanted me to go down to the slums and open a store-front ministry, I would not want to go, even if I knew it to be God's will. I pray God that I would do it, but I don't want to do it. I would rather work with the country club set. I figure that they are just as sinful, and I am more comfortable working with them. The point is that many of us mouth the words that we want God's will done, but what we really want is for God to stamp approval on our wills. It takes a pretty dedicated Christian to pray for, and mean for, God's will to be done; and to be willing to obey whatever he tells him to do. If we don't want his will done if it clashes with ours and if we are not willing to do whatever he tells us to do, then we are only "playing" at being a follower of Jesus Christ.

Some of the people who worry about whether or not they are going to Heaven haven't really thought much about what it is going to be like. Heaven is where God is, where God's will is done, where he rules. If I have spent a lifetime wanting my will done and ruling my own life, what makes me think that when I die I will want to go to Heaven? Just dying isn't going to change me. If I am completely self-centered here, just going through the physical process of dying isn't going to change anything. If Heaven is where God is, and where his will is perfectly done, then hell is separation from him. If I do not want to exist in a situation where he is the center and where he rules absolutely, then he loves me enough to let me go to hell. God never violates our freedom. It is up to me. I can either be with him, or I can separate myself from him. After all, I might not enjoy being in Heaven where he rules if I have not wanted, nor allowed, him to rule my life here on earth.

I believe that these are the three reasons why so few Christians enjoy the abundant life; as I mentioned before, they are all just variations of the one reason: WE DON'T TRUST GOD. If we trusted him, we would take chances on him; we would believe the promises of Jesus Christ, and we would want God's will done—because we know that he only wants the best for us. We know that he loves us and that the only thing blocking our enjoyment of the wonderful things he has in store for us is our distrust. We would believe, and act on that belief, that the full, exciting, happy life is the natural consequence of trusting God—who is trustworthy.

Let me try to make it as clear and definite as possible that taking a chance on God, believing the promises of Christ, and wanting God's will done is *not* the way one "gets to Heaven." This is not more law. They are not the ways you "earn" salvation. They are the ways you begin enjoying the abundant life on earth. Failure to trust him, to believe his promises, and to want his will done are blocks to the enjoyment of the abundant life, as well as failure to follow Jesus Christ as Lord and Saviour.

Actually, this can be depressing; and it is a shame that the work of Christ and the enjoyment of the life he brings goes begging because people who profess to belong to him, to be following him, and who have volunteered to serve him do not trust him. But, praise God, there is a new wind sweeping across the country—and perhaps, the world. That wind is the wind of God, the Holy Spirit. More and more people are beginning to participate in this new Pentecost that is going on. More and more are beginning to step out on faith, in trust; and they are finding that he *is* trustworthy. Christ does keep his promises; and the abundant life with all its gifts of the Holy Spirit is possible to have and enjoy here and now. People are coming to "know" God and to experience his presence and his gifts and are finding their lives changed in a glorious way. Many are experiencing the same thing that the Disciples experienced at Pentecost after the Resurrection and Ascension. They are finding out that it is all true—all the things the Bible promises, and the life Christ came to bring.

Chapter Ten
HELP MY UNBELIEF

Many people who are on the verge of getting serious about their professed commitment to Jesus Christ ask me, "How do you go about it? How do you come to trust him and follow him as Lord and Saviour? How can you make yourself believe his promises? How can you make yourself want God's will done, regardless?" It is a fact that you can *act* your way into a new kind of *thinking* more easily than you can THINK your way into a new kind of ACTING. *Commitment is a matter of the will, not the emotions.* You will yourself to trust him. You will yourself into believing his promises. You will yourself into wanting God's will done— even if emotionally you are afraid for it to happen. Many people are waiting for some emotional experience that will give them complete trust in God; and until it happens, they just continue in the same old unsatisfying, ineffective way. I believe that when you commit yourself to Jesus Christ, it is a matter of the will.

I consider that my primary job, other than as celebrant of the sacraments, is to open doors and remove blocks so that people can enjoy the benefits, and will accept the responsibilities, of being a Christian. I see myself as sort of a clerical coach and cheerleader. That is the purpose of my Teaching Missions. This is the purpose of this book. So when I am asked, "How do we do it? How do we start?" I say, first of all: PRAY for a manifestation of the Holy Spirit. Some people call this "The Baptism of the Holy Spirit," but I believe this to be a misnomer. We receive the Holy Spirit at baptism, confirmation, and in the sacraments. What we need is for us to OPEN OURSELVES so that he and his Gifts are released in our lives. I believe that every prayer is answered. We get a "yes," a "no," or a "not now" . . . but there is one prayer that we never receive a "no" answer for. That is when we ask the Holy Spirit to work in our lives. I remember the first time I ever asked the Holy Spirit to work in my life. I had a couple of little problems that I needed a little help with. It was hardly any time after that that I found myself starting college as a freshman at the age of thirty-five, the father of five children, so that I could go to seminary. THAT IS NOT WHAT I MEANT, but God often takes us at our word. He certainly did with me. Once again, let me say that I do not think that God means for every man who wants the Holy Spirit to work in his life to wind up going to seminary, nor every woman to be a missionary. Going to seminary was merely what happened to me. I believe that at baptism we are given the Holy Spirit, with all his gifts. Instead of waiting for some emotional experience, we should believe this, claim them, and then act as if we had them—*for we have.* It, too, is a matter of the will. You claim Christ's promises, act on them, and you find that you have them.

It is odd, and actually funny sometimes, how God works. Having grown up with a distasteful image of the ministry, due to my own misconception, I still dislike being called "preacher." The connotation that this word brings to me is unpleasant, undesirable, and repugnant. If you had told me fifteen years ago that I was going to be a preacher, I would have thought you were crazy, or at least a smart aleck. Even after I graduated from seminary and was sent to two little churches in south Alabama, whenever I would walk into a barbershop or store and someone would say, "Come in, Preacher," I would flinch, and almost feel like hitting him. I understood that this is an accepted custom, particularly in small towns, but it made me feel uncomfortable and slightly irritated. Although I do not like being called preacher, I love the ministry. I hope that all three of my sons decide to enter the ministry; but the point I am trying to make is that if we trust God, he does what is best for us and will work it out, even if we don't understand, or even think we want what it looks like he is calling and leading us to do and be.

So, in the process of "How do we do it?" the first thing we should do is try to open ourselves in trust to God, pray that his Holy Spirit will take over, and then OBEDIENTLY step out on faith—just a little at first. I used to say we should begin by "acting as if," but I had a man tell me one time that we had enough people "acting as if"—so, I changed it to "perform as if." Perform as if we really trusted God and believed the promises of Christ. Perform as if he really were number one in our lives, and the boss of our lives. Perform as if we really wanted his will done, even if it might clash with ours. I realize that this is a big order, I believe that the height of commitment is to be able to do this, and I also believe that it is highly doubtful that anyone can do this overnight. Usually, we have to start with one thing at a time—sometimes just a little thing—as we take our first small step in faith. When we find that God honors any effort and that he is reliable, then we can take larger steps of faith. I am firmly convinced that God will not let us down. That is why we should give thanks and praise to God in everything, because he is in charge; he has a plan for us and will work everything out for our good, even if we can't see the good in it at the time.

I do not believe that commitment is a one-time thing. I believe that we have to recommit ourselves daily. I believe that we have to die to our self-centeredness daily. As St. Paul said, "I die, daily." I think that we have to renew our commitment to Christ, and die to self, on a daily basis. I also believe that we have to ask God to give us the power to do this. This is counter to human nature, and it requires help from outside ourselves. That power is available. I am skeptical of "sawdust trail" conversions. I do not say that they cannot happen, but I think that even these are the culmination of things that have been building up for a long time. A conversion may climax at a certain point in time, but I don't believe the whole thing began and climaxed at that instant. The Christian life is a lifelong walk, and it begins with a turn. A turn away from obsession with self, a realization that one needs a saviour, and the willing acceptance of Jesus Christ as the saviour one needs. I am convinced that St. Paul's conversion was not quite as instantaneous as it reads. To me, the incident on the road to Damascus was the climax of something that had been building from his discontent with religion as he had been practicing it. His religion had not given him the satisfaction he was looking for. He was not in a personal relationship with God the way he wanted to be. That day on the Damascus road became the time and the place for St. Paul to start a new life: a life with God, a walk with God in Jesus Christ. I personally believe that the beginning of his conversion was when he heard the witness of Stephen and saw the magnificent way he died a martyr's death, praying for the forgiveness of the very people who were stoning him.

Real life with God, for us, begins when we make a conscious commitment, as an act of the will, to Jesus Christ as our Saviour—our only Saviour—and begin to allow him to be the boss of our lives. Then, we take that first tiny step in faith. We only do this when we know we need a saviour and want a different kind of life. This life must be sustained and nurtured by prayer, study, worship, the sacraments, and fellowship with others who are walking that same way.

Chapter Eleven
THE GIFT OF THE HOLY SPIRIT

This new way of living with others who are walking the same way came into being when Jesus fulfilled his promise to send the Holy Spirit to bind together, and empower, those who profess him as Lord and Saviour. The "new" people of God, the New Israel, was born as his followers met to celebrate the Jewish Feast of Pentecost.

The call to the old Israel was to serve and glorify God, and to be his instrument for the salvation of mankind. With every such "call" comes the dangers that arise out of man's inordinate pride, his self-centeredness. It is easy to remember that you are *chosen* and forget that you are *sent*. It is easy to accept that privilege is committed to you and forget that privilege carries responsibility with it. When the idea of Israel as *God's pet* prevailed, God's demands were taken lightly, and the results were inevitable. She became politically dominated by other nations, worship of God deteriorated into empty ceremony, and the mission to serve was forgotten.

Jesus regarded himself as the restorer of the call to Israel and the one who would redeem and restore Israel by the power of God. If Israel could be recalled to the true sense of her mission, then Christ could stretch forth his hands to heal and save, through his followers, to the ends of the earth. His message was rejected, and he was crucified; but before he died, Jesus implanted his mind and message in a specially chosen circle of people. On the day of Pentecost this group became the nucleus of *The Mystical Body of the Messiah,* and it went forth into the world on its mission of salvation with the authority and power of Christ himself. Because the Apostolic church believed that it had both the authorization and power to do anything that Christ could do, it did so.

Without the power and the guidance of the Holy Spirit, the church would only be an association of like-minded people with no more ability than any well-meaning group of do-gooders naturally possess. It is the work of the Holy Spirit to shape people after the image and likeness of Christ and enable them to carry on his ministry and mission. After equipping them for their task, Jesus sent his followers to GO and DO, as his representatives in and to the world. He sent the church to proclaim the Good News, witness to his ability to change lives, and bring others under his lordship.

The Holy Spirit is the enabling power who makes it possible for anyone to do anything that God calls him to— by supplying the direction and the power which otherwise would not be there. This gift is given through baptism, confirmation, and Holy Communion; but of course, God is not limited to the sacraments. He comes whenever a person surrenders his life to Jesus Christ. It is his purpose to transform us from the people we are to the people God wants, and intends, us to be. The work of the Holy Spirit is to make us holy, "fit for God," and he can work his miracle of redemption only with people who voluntarily respond and surrender. To do and be what we are called to do and be, we must allow the Holy Spirit to take over our lives.

This was necessary for the first followers of Jesus, and it is necessary for us. The Holy Spirit supplies the leadership and the power which overcomes our obsession with self, without destroying our freedom; and he makes it possible to live and work under the loving influence of Jesus Christ. When he is allowed to be in control, the kingdom of Heaven is spread; its citizens find purpose and meaning in their lives; they find comfort and are sustained in daily living; and it is finally by the power of the Holy Spirit that they shall pass through the gates of death and rise triumphant, as did Jesus Christ himself.

He does in us, through us, by us, and with us, that which God would have done—not by force, but by the persuasion of love to give ourselves back to God, as God has given himself to us in Christ. Salvation, the healing of broken relationships, bodies and minds, is what Jesus brought. He came to restore the broken relationship between God and man, and to make *whole* the bodies and minds of people, and their relationships with one another. Wherever Jesus of Nazareth went, the spirit and power of God were. After Pentecost, wherever the Disciples went, Christ and his power were. Wherever a dedicated, committed, obedient Christian goes today, Christ and his power are. This life-shaking, life-changing power produces a new kind of life. This is not comprehended by the world which does not see, or know, Christ, but to those who want it, to those who are willing to let him rule their hearts and lives—IT IS ALWAYS AVAILABLE.

He can take a listless, self-satisfied, self-centered group of in-name-only Christians and set them on fire with his Holy Spirit. The church was brought to life, and given power, to extend the work of Christ to all times and places. We are called to this work; but he will not beat us over the head, nor drag us by the scruff of the neck, into a love relationship with God and our fellowman. But if you want to be in that relationship and if you want the Holy Spirit to take over your life, he will answer your request with a life-changing "yes." The more we are willing to let him use us, change us, and even upset our lives, the more we will experience the presence and power of Christ in our lives. I have seen this happen to people time and time again as they find the resource to meet life victoriously with the peace of mind, and the direction, that gives real meaning to life. The power Christ promised is here—waiting for us to claim and use it.

As I mentioned before, I believe that there is a new Pentecost sweeping over the world. The Holy Spirit is being called upon, the gifts of the Holy Spirit are being claimed, and lives are being radically changed—and it is happening at a time when much of the world is in a worsening situation. People in all denominations are opening themselves to the Holy Spirit and offering themselves to Christ, just as the original Disciples did. They are finding that he meant it when he said, "I come that you might have life, and have it more abundantly." They know now that eternal life begins here, and is not just something you *get* "in the sweet bye and bye."

I urge you not to waste valuable time waiting for some emotional charge, some booming voice from Heaven, or some "burning bush" experience. If you have been baptized, if you accept Jesus as Lord and Saviour, you have what the original Disciples had. If the church would play the role of coach and cheerleader and instill in its members the fact that they have been chosen, called, given a task, and equipped to carry out that task—perhaps more and more of the members would step out in faith—and find that it is all true.

FAITH IS SOMETHING WE MUST USE, OR LOSE. The inactive rolls of all the churches bear witness to the fact that faith, like our arms and legs, grows lifeless without use.

This new life begins at baptism, or whenever Christ is accepted as Lord and Saviour; but if this life is not nurtured in the Christian family, buttressed by the things the church has to offer, and developed into maturity, it will deteriorate; and we will not reach out to others, step out on our faith, and put into practice the faith we profess. Our faith should force us to reach out to others in order to bring them into the new life that we are experiencing.

Chapter Twelve
THE SACRAMENTS

The sacraments are special "points of contact" between God and man. They are special points of spiritual connection through which the grace of God flows from his life into ours. Of course, this does not mean that he can only make connection with us through the sacraments. God is not limited in any way, except by our refusal to respond.

Through baptism, we enter the church by a process of initiation that establishes a unique relationship to God for all time and eternity. We do not join the church so much as we are joined into it. God takes the initiative in the sacraments. In baptism, God adopts us into his family as children and heirs—joint-heirs with his Son Jesus Christ. It is rebirth. By his gift, we are born anew: death to the old person, birth to the new person in Christ. We are made "living members of his family" by the Holy Spirit. We share his death and resurrection by baptism, and it is not only new birth but also the promise of the growth that shall be.

Baptism is something like naturalization. People can live in America and enjoy most of its benefits without being citizens—but they do not belong to the nation. They are foreigners. It is only when they are naturalized that they become members of the nation and receive all the benefits and assume all the duties of citizenship. Everyone born into the world lives in God's world. He may enjoy many of the benefits of God's kingdom, but he is not a member of the kingdom. In baptism, he is naturalized—actually, he is adopted—and becomes a citizen of God's kingdom. He is made a member of Christ's Body, a child of God and an inheritor of the kingdom. Once again, let me repeat that God is not limited by the sacraments, or anything else. Although baptism is adoption, adoption is not limited to baptism.

For those "baptized into Christ," what happens to him happens to them. Because he was resurrected, those who believe in him will be resurrected. Christians are adopted by God. As the old saying goes, "God has only one Son and no grandchildren."

In our adoption, we are given THE FAMILY NAME, Christian, and taken into God's family. We are given THE FAMILY SPIRIT. The Holy Spirit is given us to guide, empower and mold us into what we are meant to be—if we will let him. We are taken into THE FAMILY BUSINESS. There is no business like God's business, and our part in his business is to carry on the ministry of Jesus Christ, witness to his life-changing power, and try to get others to come under his Lordship. We are made coinheritors with Christ of THE FAMILY INHERITANCE—part of it now, the gifts of the Holy Spirit and enjoyment of the abundant life here on earth, and full inheritance later on, after death.

During my Teaching Missions I am often asked if I believe "once saved always saved." I do not believe this. I believe that once adopted by God, always a child of God.

In the parable, the prodigal son never stopped being a son. Even if he had chosen to remain always separated from his father, he would not have stopped being a son. Many adopted children of the Father become *prodigal* children. They have left the Father and gone off to a far land of SELF-CENTEREDNESS. They may never "come to themselves" and return to the Father. Committed children of God, by virtue of the cross and the acceptance of Jesus as their Lord and Saviour, have come to themselves, returned home, received forgiveness, and are restored to the right relationship with the Father. Unfortunately, many other adopted children may never choose to do so.

The Easter message speaks of the *resurrected life* beginning here, and continuing into eternity with Christ in the loving presence of God. We are free to leave his presence, separate ourselves from him, and remain "prodigal" children in a far-off land.

In the parable, the prodigal son came home—where the father was, where the father ruled, where the father's will was done. Heaven is where our Heavenly Father is, where he rules the hearts of his children, and where his will is done. This heavenly life with the Father begins here on earth.

There is one vital, fatal point that the "uncommitted" Christian, the disobedient child of God, overlooks or ignores: THE PRODIGAL SON WAS NOT FORCED TO COME HOME. HE MIGHT NEVER HAVE COME HOME. He was always welcome to come home—the father wanted him to come home—but he was free to choose or refuse. Had he chosen to stay away, he would have remained a son, but would have missed out on life with the father. This is how it is for some people who have been baptized, or once claimed Jesus Christ as Lord and Saviour. They became God's children, but have chosen to leave home and the Father. They may never decide to come home. They, too, are free to choose or refuse.

We who have been baptized in the name of the Father, and the Son, and the Holy Ghost are marked, forever marked, by the sign of the cross; and it is the action of the Holy Spirit who is given at baptism that moves the baptized person to seek continuing growth. In the Episcopal Church, and some others, confirmation is the sacrament of growth in the new life, of which baptism is the beginning, the birth. Confirmation provides the baptized person with the opportunity to make, under the guidance and power of the Holy Spirit, a conscious response of repentance and faith, of renunciation and obedience. Not only is confirmation more than becoming an Episcopalian, it is even more than a public profession of faith. The profession of faith and the becoming a communicant of the church are secondary to the spiritual gift of God's strengthening power, which is the purpose of "the laying on of hands." The rite of confirmation endows a person—through the action of the Holy Spirit—with POWER, the power to assume personal responsibility for his baptismal vow.

This power equips a person to take his part as a responsible partner in the family business. "The laying on of hands" is an ancient sign of the transference of power and authority. In the Old Testament, and the New, whenever God assigned a person a special task, he fitted him for that task by giving him a *special* gift of his power. In confirmation, through the laying on of hands with prayer, a special gift of God's Spirit is imparted to us—to strengthen us for meeting temptation, for living the Christian life, and for carrying on the Father's business. The prayer that accompanies "the laying on of hands" asks for the gift, with its several manifestations, in order that the person may fulfill his responsibility as a Christian. St. Paul lists these in the twelfth chapter of his first letter to the Corinthians, verses four through eleven: wisdom, knowledge, faith, gift of healing, working of miracles, prophecy, discerning of spirits, the gift of tongues, and the interpretation of tongues. Then, in the thirteenth chapter he names the greatest: love.

The sacrament of confirmation is the full initiation of the Christian into full communion in Christ's Mystical Body. The person has entered a life of grace. He has been *set apart* for a special ministry—a ministry of proclamation, witness, and service on Christ's behalf to the world. He is intended to take his rightful place in the family business, and participate fully in the life of God's family.

Chapter Thirteen
OWNER'S OPERATIONAL PLAN

Like Judaism, Christianity is therefore religion. Because God delivered the Jews and made them his people, they were supposed to be his instrument for the salvation of the world. He first proved his love for them by delivering them from bondage in Egypt. *God always proves his love before demanding anything.* Immediately before giving the Law, he recalled this fact to the Israelites. He said, "Because I showed you what kind of God I am; because I proved my love by delivering you from the hand of Pharaoh, *therefore,* thou shalt have no other gods before me. . . ." Because God, in Jesus Christ, saved us from separation from himself, because he did for us that which we could not do for ourselves, there must be a response from us. We were not only saved from something. We were also saved for something.

"Taking the Lord's name in vain" is much more than just cursing, or using his name lightly. It is a dangerous thing to ask God to damn a person, for two reasons. First, we shouldn't use the Lord's name unless we mean it. If we ask him to damn a person but do not mean it, we have taken his name in vain. If we ask him to, and mean it, then we have taken over Christ's prerogative. Only he is judge, and only he can damn someone. To ask this and not mean it is to break one of the commandments. To ask this and mean it is to usurp Christ's privilege. In either case, we stand under judgment. Another way—and a most dangerous way—of taking the Lord's name in vain is to be baptized, to be adopted and take the name "Christian," but take it in vain in that we do not fulfill our vow that we made to God at the time and do not live as obedient children of God, members of Christ's Body.

Jesus Christ came to establish a community, a family of love, acceptance, and forgiveness, where concern for one another and discipleship to him is its reason for being. He never intended to have numerous, separated units composed of just the individual and himself. Too many people want to be Christian, alone. This in itself is a contradiction in terms. We have all known people who insist that they can worship God on the golf course or while fishing just as well as in church. Of course they can, but seldom, or consistently, do. Even if they did, this is not enough. This is inadequate and unsatisfactory. Christianity means a love relationship with God which produces a love relationship with our fellowman. If Jesus himself found it necessary to worship regularly in the Temple and to live in the context of a group, such as the Disciples, I wonder why some people feel that it is not necessary for them to worship formally and participate in the life of the Christian family? Surely Jesus could have worshiped God privately and adequately —yet he found it necessary to have formal corporate worship. Many people try to operate on the principle of "just me and God" and exclude having to be bothered with other people and formal corporate worship. *This is not Christianity.* You will notice that pride enters into this, if you just look at the billing: "Me and God"; see who gets top billing. This is neither Christianity nor Judaism. This is like the hermit, or religious recluse, off in a cave or on a mountaintop. The goal is for self: to communicate with God and to receive peace of mind. This isn't Christianity; it is Eastern, Oriental mysticism. A Christian who voluntarily, and deliberately separates himself from other Christians is one who is Christian in name only, a distortion that is completely false to Christianity. Christianity means a family, a community, that is bound together under Jesus Christ and to one another by the Holy Spirit and the love of God.

At the other extreme is something that permeates *the social gospel.* It consists of "me and you," or perhaps the plural "you." WE will work things out. We will get rid of the slums, ignorance, injustice, hunger, etc.—and this is fine; but God is often left out completely. The reason for doing these things is changed. These things are being done in the name of man, instead of in the name of Jesus. This is HUMANISM, not Christianity. The only thing that makes either of these two thrusts "Christian" is my relationship to God which affects my relationship to you, in Jesus Christ. It is these relationships based on, and in obedience to, Jesus Christ that makes them Christian. The Christian must have one foot firmly planted in his relationship to Christ and the other foot firmly planted in his relationship to his fellowman. Jesus said that anyone who does not love his fellowman does not love God. To say that you love God but refuse to love your fellowman is proof that you do not love God. This is to fool yourself! The only way you can show your love for God is to express it in love for your fellow-man. We are to love our fellowman because God loves us, and him, and has commanded us to love him and our fellowman.

With respect to this, there is a block—a fact that hinders many people from really being the church. There is a difference in LIKE and LOVE, and many people confuse the two. *"Like" is entirely emotional.* We like a person because of our emotions: he agrees with us, he is interested in the same things we are, he is nice to us; or perhaps, we meet him for the first time and automatically we warm to him. There is no particular reason except that he creates a pleas-urable, emotional response in us. It is possible that we cannot explain why, but we just know that we like him. Sometimes the most likable people are scoundrels; but they have a winning personality, and we like them. Our feelings toward them are pure emotion. Of course, some forms of love are emotional also, such as *eros* and *philia;* but Christian love, *agape,* does not require emotion. *Christian love means to want, or will, the best for a person*— and the real stinger here is that *we must be willing to be used to get it for him.* Love is evidenced by action. Let's say that you are starving, and I want you to have food because I love you. If I am not willing to get you some food in one way or another, my profession of love is mere words. I can tell you over and over how much I love you, but you are going to starve to death if someone doesn't get you something to eat. Love sees to it that you get some-thing to eat, if it is physically possible.

Christian love is an act of the will. You will yourself to love people. You can love someone in the Christian way

96

without knowing him, meeting him, or having any personal feelings about him, except that you know he has a need, and you want that need filled—and you are willing to be used to get it filled. This is Christian love. Of course, the ideal situation is to like and love at the same time. This is what makes a wonderful marriage, when the two people not only love each other but like each other as well. Jesus Christ said that we should love one another. Thank God, he didn't say we had to like everyone. If he had, we would really be in a mess. I have spent a large part of my life not liking me—but I always love me. I always want the best for me, and I am willing to be used to get it for me. I am glad that Jesus did not say that we had to like everyone, because there are some people I just cannot like. You probably won't believe this, but there are some people who do not like me. I am fairly sure that Jesus did not like the people who put him on the Cross—but he loved them. He loved them enough to die for them, in order for them to have the best—a reconciliation between them and God.

There is something here that we must be careful about. This does not open up to us the dodge of saying to a person, "Well, I love you, but I don't like you." Generally speaking, if we go behind the situation, we will find that we do not like a person because "old self" is involved. They have something we wanted; they won some honor that we longed for. They are more popular than we are or more successful; or perhaps they do not appreciate just how wonderful we really are. No matter what, I am convinced that we will find that our own self-centeredness is in the background of why we do not like such-and-such a person. If you try loving them, in the Christian way of no strings, no provisions, but merely willing yourself to want the best for them—you are likely to find that the emotion of liking begins to permeate your willed act of loving. You may find that that "stinker" is not so bad after all.

To fulfill our role as disciples of Jesus Christ, we are to love as a matter of the will, to want the best for others, and to be willing to be used to get it for them. Having said this, I must also say that we cannot—and will not—do this, unless we let Christ do it through us. We have to open ourselves so that his love does the loving through us.

Some people decide to begin the Christian life in earnest, and so they immediately look around for some great deed or deeds to do. It may be that the only thing God is calling them to do at that moment is to be nice to those unpleasant people next door, or at the office—or at church. The Christian journey may have as its first step after conversion the task of being nice to your husband or wife and expressing Christian love toward your children. I am convinced that our Christianity is put to the hardest test in the nitty-gritty, everyday living and dealing with people. Many people are able to rise to the occasion for great causes and challenges, but fail in the ordinary aspects of our common life.

Yes, we were saved on that first Good Friday; but we were not only saved from something, we were saved for something. We were saved to *be* the Church, the Body of Christ, with the task of carrying on his ministry and mission to the world. We were saved to be taken into our Heavenly Father's business, much like human fathers take their offspring into the family business. There the similarity ends, because there IS no business like God's business.

Chapter Fourteen
PLAYING CHURCH?

Let me give you my definition of the Church. It is a little lengthy, and certainly not official, but I believe that it expresses what the Church is all about:

The Church is the Body of Christ, *filled* with his Spirit, *equipped* with his power, and *commissioned* to carry on his ministry to the world. It offers a ministry of reconciliation and healing. Through its sacraments, worship, and fellowship, God's Holy Spirit infuses power, guidance, love, forgiveness, and acceptance to all its members. Through its powerful witness, it attracts and compels outsiders to seek entrance. It is a loving community of concern, as people are caught up in praise and worship *of* God, and service *to* him, through its outreach and concern for the world his Son died for.

The members of the Body of Christ are people whose lives have been radically (from the roots) changed. They have received God's Holy Spirit and are using this power to change other lives and affect the world. The members are living the abundant life. They are no longer filled with guilt feelings. Anxiety, hostility, loneliness, and frustration have been erased. They love, forgive, and accept each other and are impelled to offer this same abundant life to those outside the fellowship. Members of the Body of Christ are enjoying all the benefits, and have accepted all the responsibilities, of Christianity.

Is this a description of the Church as you know it? Is it a description of the church members that you know? Is it a description of you? If it is not, it is because God has not been allowed to take over the fellowship—individually and corporately. Christ may be professed as Saviour, but he is not allowed to be Lord. If the above description of the Church does not apply to you and the rest of the congregation, it is obvious that God is not really being trusted, Christ's promises are not being believed; and the members do not want God's will to be done.

This is why many people are rejecting the organized church. They believe that most of the members are hypocrites who are merely mouthing words and going through the motions of "playing church." While this says something about their own Christianity and their understanding of the Church, their judgment is based on a great deal of truth. The organized Church is under judgment; but their dropping out, or refusing to come in, only emphasizes their lack of understanding of the Church.

The Church is no club for saints. It is a hospital for sinners—but forgiven sinners. It is a place to receive the proper medicine and therapy for individual healing, and ultimately the healing of society. We don't refuse to go to a hospital that may have hypocrites on the staff. In the business world we deal with people who are hypocrites, but some people feel that they cannot have anything to do with the Church unless it is perfect. Not only is this unrealistic and unreasonable, but it is also a hypocritical excuse on their part. Of course the Church is not perfect; otherwise I wouldn't be allowed in, and not too many other people would be either. The Church is made up of people who know they need a saviour and profess that Jesus Christ is their Saviour and Lord. If they will allow him to, he will transform them into a new kind of people, a "third race." Sometimes this is a slow process because other things distract us. We have not yet completely died to our self-centeredness, but this is more apt to happen in the company of others who have taken the first step than in any other place.

As people begin to mature in the new life Christ offers, they begin to experience some fulfillment of his promises; and this encourages them to tell others—and show others—and invite others to come in. They want other people to come into this love relationship with God, to join in the family life of God's people.

All too often, the Church is thought of as being "over there, somewhere." This is a complete misconception. The Church is anywhere a Christian is: where he works, where he plays, where he goes. The Church has two aspects: THE GATHERED and THE SCATTERED, and both aspects are made up of the same people.

THE GATHERED CHURCH exists to do two things: worship God and train for mission. It needs to worship God out of duty of creature to Creator, out of love of forgiven sinner towards a loving, forgiving Heavenly Father. There, it gathers strength, knowledge, and guidance through prayer, study, the sacraments, and fellowship so that the purpose of the Scattered Church can be fulfilled. To worship God and train for mission is why the Church gathers.

THE SCATTERED CHURCH exists for the purpose of carrying out that mission. These are the only reasons for the existence of the Church: worship, training for mission, and carrying the mission out. The church is not missions, it is mission. *The Church is the apostolic community,* one that is "sent." Many people think that mission means something we do *to* or *for* those poor starving heathens "over there, somewhere." It is that; but the mission of the Church may also be one-half block down the street, next door, in the office, or across the breakfast table. The mission of the Church *is* across the world; but it is also IN and TO your family, neighbors, friends, and fellow workers. It is to the best educated, richest, nicest person you know, but no less to the least educated, poorest, biggest heel you know. You, as the Church, may be the only person God can use to reach that one person you personally cannot stand. And if you do not reach him, he may spend this life, and the life to come, separated from God.

Few people will argue with the first purpose of the Gathered Church—to worship God; but all too many want to stop there. Many do stop there, and the Church becomes their little club. When I stop there, the Church becomes something that exists for ME—to make me feel better, to give me comfort and strength, to have my sins forgiven—ALL FOR ME, or the corporate "me," US. This is only part of the Church's purpose, and we dare not stop there. When we do—IT CEASES TO BE THE CHURCH. It may be pleasant, it may be comfortable, it may be a haven, but it is not the Church. People who allow the Church to stop there, and become an exclusive club for its members, become "sick unto death" and eventually die. The danger of this happening is a constant threat. Because this has been allowed to happen, the cause of Jesus Christ has been seriously hampered. As one who loves the Episcopal Church, I have to admit that this is a particular danger, and a common occurrence, in many of our parishes. One of the purposes of the Holy Spirit is to "stir up" the members of the Church, and almost "drive" them out into the world on Christ's mission and ministry. If they do not allow him to do this, then their reason for existence dies; and their worship of God is empty, meaningless, and futile.

Sometimes people confuse the second purpose of the Gathered Church with *busyness*. They act as though they believe that if the Church will cook enough spaghetti suppers, polish enough brass, and put on enough bazaars, the second purpose of the Gathered Church will be accomplished. These, and other things like them, are good and often necessary; but they are not "training for mission." We should test our busyness. We should ask ourselves: "Does everything that is done by, and in, the Church pertain to one of these two purposes of the Gathered Church? By doing them are we worshiping God or training for mission?" If not, then we need to take a closer look at the activities of the Gathered Church. Fellowship is vital. The kingdom of God is not only within us, it is among us. Christ said that when two or three were gathered in his name, he would be there; but there is a great deal more to the Church than just fellowship.

"Training for mission" means Bible study, prayer groups, witnessing groups, study courses, Christ-oriented encounter

103

groups, Sunday school, and the like. As we grow and learn what the Church is, and what it is supposed to do, we begin to receive our directions as God's people and his instruments. The Risen Lord made the church the instrument through which his saving power is to be made known and his saving purpose accomplished. He gave it a commission, and the equipment to carry out his mission. He expects that mission to be accomplished. The Church is his *representative* in and to the world.

Church attendance is not enough. It may be the tip-off on the depth of commitment—because committed members attend church regularly; but not all regular church attenders are "committed." There are people who attend church regularly, but never go to Sunday school, or attend Bible classes, or study courses. There are some who attend Sunday school, but seldom go to church services. This is not only unfortunate, it is detrimental to their spiritual health, and to Christ's cause. Church services are worship of God. Sunday school is learning about God. Neither is a substitute for the other. Commitment to Jesus Christ is deepened, nurtured, and guided by fellowship, study, and prayer. A congregation where there are no prayer groups, study courses, and Bible classes is almost inevitably a congregation where commitment is shallow, attendance is small and sporadic, and the outreach is almost nil. The Gathered Church is where Christians are to be nurtured and trained so that as they mature spiritually, attendance increases, giving of time and money increases, and involvement and concern with and for other people becomes meaningful and commonplace. Christianity is a way of life. It is a continuing journey where those involved mature spiritually and responsibly. The Church is composed of new people—people made new by the Holy Spirit, living the new life, and sent out upon their task in the power of the Holy Spirit.

The Scattered Church has the task of carrying out the mission that it has been trained for. It is made up of the called-out who live the new life in the world. That mission is summed up in one word, a word that terrifies many people—especially Episcopalians. They turn pale, break out in a cold sweat, and draw back as if you had slapped them. Nevertheless, the Scattered Church exists to—WITNESS.

Many people have been turned off by this word because it has a history of being abused or distorted. Many times their *witness* has come across as a witness against the Christian life. This is unfortunate, since the business of the Scattered Church is witnessing.

Chapter Fifteen
SELLING THE PRODUCT

EVERYONE WITNESSES. We have no choice in the matter. We cannot sit on the sidelines and say, "I'll do everything but that." We either witness to the life-changing power of Jesus Christ, or we witness against him as a life-changer. We witness to the fact that he has made a difference in our lives, or we witness to the fact that he has not made a difference in them. There is no choice in the matter of whether or not we will witness. The only choice is whether we witness for him or against him. Christianity has never been a spectator sport. When Christians try to make it one, or try to be just a spectator, they become a witness against the life-changing power of Jesus Christ. Unfortunately, many Christians lead lives that do not witness to this power; and their profession of following Jesus is a lie or a charade. They have taken the Lord's name in vain. They are traitors to him as Lord; they practice treason against his cause, and are AWOL from his army most of the time. Because this is true for so many people who have voluntarily enlisted in his army, Christianity's effectiveness has been seriously hampered. Apathy and arrogance are the greatest threats to the cause of Christ. Apathy toward the vow each Christian makes, and arrogance, as man exalts himself and relegates God to the position of "The Man Upstairs," are evidence that man is rebuilding the Tower of Babel. The builders of the original Tower of Babel did not get away with it, and I do not believe the modern builders will either.

If Jesus died that all might be saved, then why witness? Yes, it is true that he died for everyone; but his death is only effective for obedient, penitent believers. Dietrich Bonhoffer, the great twentieth-century martyr who practiced what he preached, once said, "Only he who believes is obedient, and only he who is obedient believes." Being obedient doesn't necessarily mean that we will enjoy it. I once made the statement, in an adult Sunday school class, that we did not have to enjoy being obedient. For one man it was the most enlightening and helpful thing he had ever heard, other than the fact that salvation was a gift and not something that is earned. He spent a large amount of time working around the church, but sometimes he resented doing so when there were other things he had rather be doing. This was particularly true on Saturdays, when he preferred to listen to football games as he worked in his basement trying to complete a couple of rooms that his family needed badly. He felt guilty because he was not particularly enjoying his work around the church: cutting grass, repairing, and painting. He thought that as a Christian he should enjoy doing these odd jobs that need to be done, but were keeping him from doing some things he wanted to do around his house—and he felt guilty for resenting them. He found great relief when I told him that being obedient to what he believed God wanted him to do was the important thing—not whether or not he enjoyed doing it. Fitting in with this is the fact that God does not require that we be successful, only that we be obedient. Successful results, in any Christian endeavor, are in God's department. We have only to be obedient.

When I accepted Jesus Christ as my Lord and Saviour, God adopted me. Nothing can ever change that. I am forever his child, but like the prodigal son in the parable, I am free to separate myself from him. I am also free to return home to him.

On the cross, Jesus bought my ticket to Heaven. When I accepted Jesus, I picked up that ticket. I am free to remain on the bus. I am free to get off the bus. God never violates our freedom. In order to enjoy eternal life with the Father, now and later on, I must be with the Father. If I have deliberately separated myself from him, I must "come to myself" and return to him and live under his rule. My discovering this vital fact may be dependent upon somebody, somewhere, telling me this and showing me the joy of life with Father.

The Gospel according to St. John has as its two emphases: Love one another and stay in the Body. These two, along with Christ's command to be his witness, are what Christianity is all about. If Christianity were only concerned with "the sweet bye and bye," perhaps there might not be as great a need to witness; but ETERNAL LIFE BEGINS HERE ON EARTH. The kingdom of Heaven begins here on earth; life in the love relationship with God our Heavenly Father begins here on earth; and there are millions of people who are existing in hell right here on earth. They are living lives that are meaningless, filled with guilt, anxiety, and despair. They have separated themselves from the love and power of God. They are floundering in a vain attempt to be self-sufficient, seeking after false saviours, with values based on the world's standards. They are unhappy, frustrated, and mixed-up. There are others who are not as desperate—merely dissatisfied, unfulfilled, and vaguely discontented. None of this is necessary. This is what Jesus came to do away with.

Christ has made possible a new kind of life: the abundant life; and this is why the need to witness is so great—and urgent. If you were drastically ill with some incurable disease and some doctor with a wonderful medicine came along and healed you, no one would have to tell you to tell people about this doctor with his wonderful medicine. You couldn't wait to tell others. Christ offers the only help, the only cure, that will keep our lives from being empty, meaningless, and filled with guilt, anxiety, and despair. The world needs desperately to know about this. This is what the person next door, the couple with the marriage problems, the alcoholic, the guilt-ridden man at the office needs to hear. This may be what someone in your own family needs to know. Heaven can wait. Eternal Life begins here on earth. People need to know that it is possible to live the resurrected life NOW. We are loved, forgiven, and accepted—and we do not deserve it. Jesus Christ provides the power for us to offer this same love, forgiveness, and acceptance to others—ALL OTHERS. We cannot do this on our own; our human, self-centered nature keeps getting in the way; but through Jesus Christ we can. This new way of living is possible, and available, to all people—and they need to know it.

Let's say that you have an uncle over in Australia, and he dies and leaves you one million dollars. You are now worth a million dollars; but if no one ever tells you about it, and you do not claim it—IT CANNOT AFFECT YOUR LIFE IN ANY WAY. Because of the death of your uncle, you now have access to resources that can give you a completely new way of living: a life so different that it is almost beyond your wildest dreams. I realize that it is not always good to inherit money, and I know that it is possible to inherit a million dollars and ruin your life—but what I am saying is that if you are not told about it and you do not claim it, it cannot have *any* effect—good or bad—on your life. It is exactly the same with the Good News of Jesus Christ. If people are not told, and if they do not claim what is theirs —even though all its benefits are theirs—it can have no effect on them and their lives. What good is it if we do not know about it and do not claim it? THIS IS THE REASON CHRIST COMMANDED US TO BE HIS WITNESSES.

God reaches people through *believing Christians* who have *experienced* this new life: the love, joy, and power that Christ offers. Christianity is just like "show and tell" in the first grade of school. People need to be told, and shown, what it is that Christ has done for them and now offers them. *It cannot be words only.* Words alone will convince no one. I remember attending a conference once where one lady spent most of her time saying that she loved everybody and that she had Jesus in her heart. Her husband was an alcoholic, and there is a good possibility that she drove him to it. She and her children did not get along with one another; yet she insisted that she loved everybody and had Jesus in her heart. Based on the impression she gave to people, I wouldn't believe her if she swore it on a stack of Bibles. It is my "Christian evaluation" that she was merely mouthing words. If the life we lead does not match the words we say, our witness is meaningless—and can be detrimental to the cause of Christianity—because it is a witness against the life-changing power of Jesus Christ. Our lives can cancel our words.

The other half of "show and tell" brings us to the ever-popular Episcopal excuse. I have heard so many Episcopalians say, "I don't need to say anything. I just want people to look at me, and my life will be a witness." What this really means is that they are sort of "chicken." If this is all they ever do, people may think that they are just good Hindus, or atheists, or maybe that they were just born nice people. People who do this are witnesses to themselves. A Christian witness is one who witnesses to the fact that Jesus Christ has changed him—or has enhanced whatever good qualities he had before he knew him. If you are called to be a witness in court, you can't just get up on the witness stand and look like a witness. There comes a time when you have to open your mouth and say something. Of course, having something to say that you know, or believe, personally and knowing what to say, and when to say it, makes all the difference in the world as to whether or not your witness will be effective.

There are Christians who turn people off—either in their approach or by the fact that their lives do not match their words. This certainly does nothing to further the spread of Christianity. There is a time to speak and a time to keep quiet, and anyone who allows the Holy Spirit to rule his life will know which is which. People are funny in that overzealousness can come over as phoniness to them. When this happens, instead of convincing people or attracting people, it may cause them to resist and to consider the person who is *witnessing* to be a "religious nut."

I remember when I was a teen-ager, a traveling evangelist who came to town with his own tent. He really packed the people in—so much so that one of the local churches called him to be its pastor. This man was good looking, sharp, and quite a salesman. He was instrumental in bringing many people to the point of committing their lives to Jesus Christ. Some of these people might not have been reached by any other approach than his. Several young men who seemed unlikely prospects entered the ministry, the missionary field, or into some kind of full-time church work. I praise God for this. He had a great influence on many teen-agers, but some of them were inclined to overdo things. He had them standing in front of the local theater begging people not to go to the movies on Sundays. This was the time when theaters were just beginning to open on Sundays in the South. I am not sure that these young people prevented anyone from entering, but I am sure that their method was offensive to many people. I do know that this is not what I am talking about when I say that we are called by Jesus Christ to witness. I had taught tap dancing off and on since I was around eleven years old. Of course, this evangelist preached against dancing, along with many, many other things. At school some of these overzealous teen-agers would corner me and try to convince me that dancing was sinful. I didn't buy that either; and as hard as money was to come by in the 1930s, they had latched on to the wrong boy. This only served to reinforce my idea that if this was what Christianity was, then "thanks, but no thanks."

I still remember the times that I would be walking down the street and some recent convert would buttonhole me and want to know if I had found Jesus. I felt like saying, "Is he lost again?" I knew this was just a reaction against their method, and I believe that this is a distortion of what Jesus meant with his command to be his witness. It seems to me that this kind of witness can produce negative feelings toward what they think is Christianity. I certainly saw nothing attractive about the Christian life in these people and their approach to Christian discipleship.

A life that matches the words, a life that exhibits joy and peace of mind, a person who seems to be living the abundant life—this is what reaches people. Changed lives, that are obviously changed for the better, lives that exhibit the power of Christ in them, are what attract other people into taking a chance on Jesus Christ. It seems to me that Christians should manifest something that makes other people say, "I don't know what it is that you've got—but I want it." There are millions of lonely, guilt-ridden, anxious people crying out for forgiveness, love, understanding, and acceptance. They are crying out for a different kind of life from the one they are living at present. If Christians can show, as well as tell, them about what they themselves have found, the life that Jesus Christ offers, and tell them that it can be theirs as well—they will eagerly reach out for it and praise God that someone told them about it. Christianity *is* truly caught more than it is taught. Christians are supposed to be contagious and to go around infecting everyone. It has been said that many Christians

113

have been innoculated with just enough Christianity so that it never takes; they never develop a good case of it. Unfortunately, this seems to be true for many people. Praise God, there ARE people today who are "breaking out" in full-blown cases of Christianity, and they are infecting more and more people.

Chapter Sixteen

RECRUITMENT PROGRAM

This is why the Church is mission. Those who know about it, and are experiencing it, have a commission from Jesus Christ to show and tell others that this wonderful gift is theirs—if they will only accept it. People need to know that there is available a power that will enable them to live victoriously within the tensions of this world and that it has been communicated to the Church with the coming of the Holy Spirit. This power and this new life are available to anyone who is willing to turn his life over to Jesus Christ. When he does so, he is privileged to claim this power and act upon it. When this happens, he finds that the promise of Jesus is fulfilled in his life, and he has begun to live the abundant life that Jesus spoke of.

The point of Christianity's message is not so much that we have a choice between Heaven and hell after we die, but that we can choose to enter the kingdom of Heaven now—and it will continue for eternity. This is what the parable of the vineyard is telling us.

You remember the parable: A man had a crop that needed harvesting, and so he left his farm to hire some workers. The picture that comes to my mind whenever I read this parable is one that is familiar from my youth. I think about the small towns where there are some men who just sit around the courthouse yard whittling, talking, laughing, chewing tobacco, and killing time. The man comes to them and tells them that he will pay them five dollars if they will come and help him harvest his crop. Some of them go with him and begin working around eight o'clock that morning. Around eleven o'clock the man realizes that he needs more workers, so he returns to the courthouse yard to hire some. Some more agree to go to work when he promises that he will treat them right at the end of the day. Around two o'clock in the afternoon he sees that he needs still more men, so once again he goes to recruit workers and makes the same agreement with them. Then, at five o'clock—one hour before quitting time—he hires some other men, promising them also that he will treat them right at quitting time. When it comes time to pay off, he gives those who had worked since eight o'clock that morning five dollars, but then he gives all the others the same amount. I am sure that this is one of the parables less favored by labor unions. Naturally those who had worked all day complained; but the man said, "Did I not pay you what I promised you? Why do you complain if I am generous to these other men?"

The most important point of this parable is that everybody gets the same thing. Theologically, it means that God cannot give us 10 percent of eternal life. You either get the whole bundle, or nothing. There are people who resent *deathbed conversions*. They figure that if they have to work, and "give up" doing what they really want to do, then it is not fair for some one to "come to Jesus," as they say, at the last moment, and get to go to Heaven also. They are still hung-up on earning salvation. They are like the men in the parable who grumbled at the generosity of the farmer. To feel this way is to miss the important point that the Christian life, working with and for the Master, is satisfying and exciting—not restrictive.

There is a second important point in this parable that is often overlooked, but vital to the understanding of the Christian life: anyone who has worked for Christ most of his life would not begrudge people who come in at the last minute. He would only be sorry that they had not come in earlier. He knows that *real living* is life with Christ and that drifting along doing just as one pleases is not the wonderful thing that some people think it would be. Doing just as one pleases can be the least satisfying of any kind of life. Those who come into the right relationship with God and get just a taste of what working for Christ is like, would not gloat to others over the fact that they "got in" at the last minute. They would regret every moment they had wasted before coming in.

Until those who profess to be followers of Jesus Christ exhibit what real living is or until they discover what real Christian living is, they are going to continue thinking and acting as if Heaven is something in the sweet bye and bye, a reward for giving up what one really wants to do. As long as this is the witness they give, people will never be attracted to the idea of wanting to "work for the Master."

Christians should be walking advertisements for the Christian life. Jesus Christ is in the life-changing business. That business has been handed on to his followers. Christ is the one who changes lives, but he needs workers in the fields to introduce them to him. The only thing that is going to attract people to the Church and the Christian life is to see the effect of his life-changing on the people who profess to belong to him. People must be able to see his influence on his followers in the way they face trouble, the way their faith affects their everyday lives, and the way their commitment to Jesus Christ affects their relationships and dealings with other people.

Evangelism is any activity to induce others to commit their lives to Jesus Christ. This is God's business that he has given to the Church through Jesus Christ. I believe that any judgment that Christians face will be based on how we have handled his business. This will not be a judgment on whether we will be damned or not. That judgment took place on Good Friday, and we were found guilty. But Christ the Judge took the penalty on himself, and we have been acquitted. I Corinthians 3:1-15 speaks to this, but at the same time speaks of another judgment that we face.

According to the grace of God given to me, like a skilled master builder I laid a foundation, and another man is building upon it. Let each man take care how he builds upon it. For no other foundation can any one lay than that which is laid, which is Jesus Christ. Now if any one builds on the foundation with gold, silver, precious stones, wood, hay, straw—each man's work will become manifest; for the Day will disclose it, because it will be revealed with fire, and the fire will test what sort of work each one has done. If the work which any man has built on the foundation survives, he will receive a reward. If any man's work is burned up, he will suffer loss, though he himself will be saved (I Cor. 3:10-15).

Christians will face a judgment of a sort: a judgment on what we have done with the work Christ has given us to do. That work is the edifying, the building up, of the Church. It concerns the Lordship of Jesus Christ. This judgment that we face will be based on two questions: First, "Have I allowed Jesus Christ to be the Lord, the Boss, of my life?" Second, "What have I done to get others to come under his Lordship?"

Have I allowed him to change my life? Have I influenced anyone else to let him change his life? These are what this judgment that we will face one day will be based on. As far as I am concerned, I believe that judgment day will consist of one word from God. As each of us stands before him, he will say, "Well?" . . . and then it will be our time to speak.

I wonder if you would know what I was talking about if I were to ask you what a "time step" is? Do you know what "Shuffle off to Buffalo" means? Back in the days of vaudeville, no matter what a person's act was—he knew how to do the time step and how to "Shuffle off to Buffalo." These two things are a couple of steps in tap dancing. One is the beginning, and the other is the exit step. No matter what your act might be, you made sure that you knew how to do a few steps of tap dancing to use in case of an emergency. If you were a juggler, a magician, tumbler, or what have you, and something went wrong—you dropped your prop or something else happened—you couldn't just stand there with hundreds of people looking at you, and you were *dead* if you just walked off the stage. So, you started doing the time step and worked your way off stage with "Shuffle off to Buffalo."

I believe that on judgment day when Christ says, "Well?"

119

a lot of people had better know how to do the time step and "Shuffle off to Buffalo." Many of us will not be able to stand there under the piercing gaze of our Judge. What legitimate excuse can we offer him for not doing, and being, what he intended us to do and be? What possible excuse will stand up if we have failed to take care of our part in God's business?

The commitment of all too many church members is exceedingly shallow. The element of sin, the obsession to have one's own way, constantly dilutes the work of the Church. Think of the people who leave a church because they do not like the minister or certain lay leaders. Many people leave the Church because of what the National Council of Churches or their own National Headquarters is doing. I have known people to leave their church because of certain Sunday school material. The Episcopal Church has many who are leaving it because of the new trial liturgy. There may be a reason to leave a particular church, but to withdraw from *The Church* is inexcusable. This is one of the principal things that the gospel and epistles of St. John warn us against. I have heard Episcopalians say, "I am not going back to Church until they get rid of 'The Green Book' trial liturgy." I do not believe that God will accept that type of thing as an excuse for failing to let Jesus Christ be Lord, as well as Saviour. I do not believe he will accept that kind of self-centered excuse for withdrawing from the fellowship of other Christians. What if a person dies before they bring back the 1928 Prayer Book? What if a person dies before his church calls a different minister? What if a person dies before those people he does not like move away? Christians are supposed to be

120

willing to die for the cause of Christ, and yet an awful lot of people are not willing to endure a minister they do not like, certain procedures they do not approve of, or a trial change in the way they have been worshiping. This sort of thing is a blot on the witness of people in all denominations.

A real part of the "call" of Christ is the possibility of having to suffer for him. It seems to me that most Christians not only are not willing to suffer—they are not willing to be inconvenienced. I am afraid that the commitment of the majority of Christians corresponds to the old joke about the boy who told his girlfriend that he would fight dragons, swim oceans, climb mountains for her . . . and that he would be over Friday night, if it didn't rain. It is this kind of lukewarm commitment that many people are going to have to try to explain when they stand before the Judge, and he says, "Well?"

If enough people attend one of my Teaching Missions or read this book—and "buy" what I am saying—it may bring back tap dancing as they storm the dance studios in order to learn how to do the time step and "Shuffle off to Buffalo." I am glad that I learned how to tap dance many years ago.

Chapter Seventeen
AN OLD/NEW WIND BLOWING

Perhaps the reason the Church seems to fail so often, and sometimes appears to be ineffective, is that it contains so many in-name-only Christians who have never known Jesus Christ. They have never had any kind of encounter with him and have never verbally and consciously committed their lives to him. There is a built-in danger in denominations that baptize infants. Unless the child's parents, and his church family, teach the Christian faith and stress the need for a personal commitment to Jesus Christ, he may grow up with only a lukewarm faith. Unless he one day makes a personal commitment, he is liable to miss the benefits and shirk the responsibilities of Christian discipleship. He needs to know that this dedication is necessary and that God provides the power to fulfill it. Because only lip service is given, in many cases, to something that really means a life commitment, all too many people seem to wind up "playing church." God's business is hindered and lives go unchanged because the commitment that is the driving force behind the mission and ministry of the Body of Christ is missing.

Faith is action based on commitment to whatever it is we

believe in. This is true for secular things as much as it is for religious matters. People always express their commitment to whatever they believe in—and they do it by word and deed. This is true whether it be a political party, alumni association, or Jesus Christ. Faith is ACTION based on COMMITMENT to WHATEVER it is that we BELIEVE in.

Christ commanded us to be his witnesses, but *one cannot witness to something one has not seen or experienced.* If there is a car wreck and you did not see it, or were not in it, then you cannot be a witness concerning it. All you can possibly say is that you heard that there was a wreck; some people said that there was a wreck; and you can see evidence of a wreck—but you cannot be a witness, because you did not see it happen. Everything about it is secondhand information, as far as you are concerned. Much of the Church is dealing with secondhand information concerning Jesus Christ. So many churchgoers have not experienced an encounter with him; and the most they can say is that the Bible says so and so, and some people say so and so, and they see evidence of changed lives; but—they themselves have nothing of a firsthand nature to witness to. And, THEY NEVER WILL—so long as they hold on to their private gods and saviours.

So long as people refuse to surrender their lives to the Lordship of Jesus Christ; so long as they are afraid to trust God and to believe the promises of Jesus, and to want God's will done in their lives, if it clashes with their wills, then they are not apt to have much of anything to witness to. This is where many people are right now. Many clergymen are also dealing with secondhand information. Unfortunately, many of them have never really committed their lives to the Lordship of Jesus Christ and have never had any kind of encounter with him. If this is true—and I honestly believe so—then how can they "sell" anyone else on taking a chance on God?

As long as people put other things first and refuse to surrender their lives to Christ, they will see little difference in their lives. There are people who will tell you that Christianity is ineffective, the Church is irrelevant, and its claims and promises a fraud. One should never knock something unless one has tried it; and many people, many Christians, have never really tried Christianity. They have confused Christianity with "churchianity," and these are not necessarily the same thing. Would that churchianity were always Christianity.

The *New Wind* that I earlier said was sweeping through the organized Church today is really the "old wind" that is the Spirit of God. His Spirit seems to be gaining momentum, as it has at other times in history, and is today having an exciting, exhilarating effect on the world. Lives are being changed; Jesus Christ is being experienced; and power is being received, claimed, and used perhaps as never since the Pentecost that the Book of Acts tells of. In one sense, this is the most exciting time to be alive since the first century of Christianity. Some people think this is fulfillment of the prediction of what will happen in the last days. More and more people are finding that the promises of Christ are true. They are finding them fulfilled in their lives, and the lives of other people. All over the world, in all Christian denominations, there are ever enlarging groups of people who seem to be like the first-century Christians that the Bible speaks of. These people are having their lives changed radically, and they are finding out what the abundant life really is.

If your life is less than completely satisfying, if your religion is not joyful, powerful, and exciting—perhaps now is the time for a change. The vocation of every Christian is to be a witness to Jesus Christ, a partner with God, and an instrument of the Holy Spirit in the life-changing business of being the Church. We are called upon to operate as Christians—no matter how we earn our living. Earning our living is our job, but our business is one of helping to conduct God's business. God wants us as junior partners in his business. When his business is operated according to his instructions and by his power, it is an exciting operation. It requires a pretty heavy investment on our part—our lives; but the dividends are overwhelming. When we invest our lives in it, our standards of living rise to new heights, the quality of our coworkers is first rate, and the retirement benefits cannot be beaten.

Chapter Eighteen
OPENINGS AVAILABLE

Anyone planning to enter any business, or to become active in a firm he has been taken into, should learn as much about it as he can, in order to be successful. It is important that he know its history, the official business terms, its assets and its liabilities and its method of operation. He should be aware of its highest potential, and the pitfalls to be avoided. He should be well informed on the immediate benefits as well as the long-range ones, but most of all he should know the PRODUCT and his BOSS. People who join a firm uninformed, and remain that way, never avail themselves of all the benefits nor do they become successful, productive members of the organization. It is also possible for people who have inherited a business to lose the business through ignorance, apathy, or poor business acumen.

It is no different with God's business. Some of you who read this book may be potential members of the firm, and future inheritors of the business. Others may have already joined the firm, are inheritors of the business, but are not active participants in conducting it. In either case, this book is directed toward you.

The most important fact that must be understood is that working for the owner of this business brings immediate benefits that cannot be earned. The moment one joins the firm, he automatically becomes an inheritor of the total assets—a down payment now, plus a guarantee of the entire stock upon maturity. This stock is a gift with dividends that increase as the initial down payment is used in conjunction with the person's dedication to the goals that the owner has set up for the benefit of the stockholders. Eternal Life in the kingdom of God is the inheritance. The gift of the Holy Spirit is the down payment. The abundant life that Christ gives is life as an active partner in God's business. The owner of the business started the business for the benefit of anyone who wants to join the firm. He himself is constantly available for guidance, strength, and comfort. He resides in his plant, the Church. Like the workers in the parable of the vineyard, the "good life" is found in working for the owner. He calls us to this work—this Life in his kingdom. There is nothing that can prevent us from enjoying all his blessings, except our own desire to be boss, or our lack of interest in the business he has made for us. Life away from the owner, either as one who refuses to come into the firm, or as one, like the prodigal son, who rejects living and working under the boss, is life that has missed its mark. At best, that life is less than satisfying, fulfilling, and joyful, and at its worst is meaningless, empty, anxious, frustrating, hopeless, and terrifying.

Jesus Christ said, "I am the way, the truth and the life." Each person has, or will have, a chance to make his choice of what kind of life he wants. Only a fool, or a gambler, can hope for success in a business that he has no

127

faith in, a product he does not believe in, and an owner he does not trust.

It is true! There is no business like God's business, like no business I know. The Church is the hiring hall with a sign saying, "Partners wanted, inquire within." I urge you to give some serious thought to taking an opening in this exciting business, or to rededicating your life to the business you joined at your baptism, or whenever you accepted Christ as Lord and Saviour. I guarantee that you will find out how exciting and satisfying it can be, working for the world's greatest boss, in the world's greatest business—God's business.